OUTSPOKEN

ROLE MODELS

FROM THE

LESBIAN AND GAY

COMMUNITY

MICHAEL THOMAS FORD

MORROW JUNIOR BOOKS

NEW YORK

For June Steffensen Hagen and Marilyn Mollenkott—for teaching me the beauty and strength of not being silent. And for James Garcia—for staying up with me all night when it was time to open the closet door.

Published by Morrow Junior Books
A division of William Morrow and Company, Inc.
1350 Avenue of the Americas, New York, NY 10019
www.williammorrow.com

Printed in the United States of America.

1   2   3   4   5   6   7   8   9   10

Library of Congress Cataloging-in-Publication Data
Ford, Michael Thomas.
Outspoken: role models from the lesbian and gay community
Michael Thomas Ford.
p. cm.
Collection of interviews with women and men who are lesbian and
gay. Summary: Gay men and lesbians describe their personal experiences
and how their sexual orientation has affected their lives. Includes lists
of recommended books, magazines, movies, and other sources of
information.
ISBN 0-688-14896-4
1. Gay men—United States—Interviews—Juvenile literature.   2. Lesbians—
United States—Interviews—Juvenile literature.   [1. Gay men.
2. Lesbians. 3. Homosexuality.]   I. Title.
HQ76.2.U5F65 1998   305.9'0664—dc21   97-40576   CIP AC

CONTENTS

Author's Note   5

LESBIAN AND GAY FAST FACT #1
What Does It Mean to Be Lesbian or Gay?   7

Alison Bechdel: Cartoonist   10

LESBIAN AND GAY FAST FACT #2
Why Are Some People Gay or Lesbian?   25

Mark Leduc: Olympic Silver Medalist in Boxing   29

LESBIAN AND GAY FAST FACT #3
How Many Gay People Are There?   45

Nancy Garden: Writer   48

LESBIAN AND GAY FAST FACT #4
How Do I Know If I'm Gay or Lesbian?   70

Dan Butler: Actor   73

LESBIAN AND GAY FAST FACT #5
What Is Homophobia?   87

Sarah Pettit: Magazine Editor   92

LESBIAN AND GAY FAST FACT #6
Don't All Lesbians Look Like Truck Drivers,
and Don't All Gay Men Like Ballet?   106

Dr. Martin Palmer: Doctor   109

LESBIAN AND GAY FAST FACT #7
Don't All Gay People Get AIDS?   124

Jenifer Levin: Mother and Writer   127

LESBIAN AND GAY FAST FACT #8
Don't Most Religions Say That Being Gay Is
Wrong?   140

Rabbi Lisa Edwards: Spiritual Leader   143

LESBIAN AND GAY FAST FACT #9
What Does "Coming Out" Mean?   165

Kevin Jennings: Educator   168

LESBIAN AND GAY FAST FACT #10
I Want to Come Out, But How Do I Do It?   190

Tim Gill: Business Executive   193

LESBIAN AND GAY FAST FACT #11
How Do I Find Other Gay Young People?   207

Sgt. Edgar Rodriguez: Police Officer   209

For Further Information   235

Index   238

AUTHOR'S NOTE

This book is a collection of interviews with women and men who are lesbian and gay. Just as the world is made up of many different kinds of people, so, too, is the community to which all these people belong. They each have their own ideas and their own opinions. Sometimes they agree; sometimes they don't.

One of the things about which there are many different opinions is what people in this community call themselves. To some, the term *gay community* includes gay men, lesbians, bisexuals, and transgendered people. To some, it means only gay men. Some people like to use the term *lesbian and gay community*, while others believe that still leaves out bisexual and transgendered people.

All of this can be very confusing. So to keep things simple, I will use the terms *gay community* or *lesbian and gay community* in this book. When I use those terms, I am including bisexual people, lesbians, transgendered people, gay men, and anyone else who feels that they are a part of this diverse community. Until we come up with a term that includes all of the different kinds of people in our community, this will have to do.

You will also see the word *queer* used in this book. This word has often been used to express hatred of people in the gay and lesbian community. But many gay people have now chosen to take back that word and use it to describe themselves. They feel that because *queer* means *different,* it is a good word to describe all of the unique kinds of people who make up the gay community. So when you see some of the people in the book using the word, remember that they are saying it with pride.

LESBIAN AND GAY FAST FACT **ONE**

What Does It Mean to Be Lesbian or Gay?

When someone is gay or lesbian, basically this means that the person is attracted to other people of the same sex in the same way that nongay people are attracted to people of the opposite sex. But this is a very simple definition, and it leaves out several things.

The easiest way to understand what being gay means is to think about what we are taught about how people love one another. When we're little, we know that boys and girls "like" one another. As we get older, we see that boys and girls go on dates and hold hands and kiss. Eventually, they are expected to get married, and perhaps to have children. Most people grow up hoping that one day they will meet someone they love and with whom they want to share their lives.

This is what we see every day—on television and in motion pictures, in romance novels and in magazines. We see ads for products that promise to make us irresistible to the opposite sex. We talk to our friends about who we think is attractive, and whom we'd like to date.

But not every boy wants to date girls, and not every girl marries a boy. Some boys want to marry other boys; some girls fall in love with other girls. And some people fall in love with both boys and girls.

Being lesbian or gay means that you are not doing things the way most of the people around you are probably doing them. It means that maybe there is a girl whose smile turns you on, but you are a girl, too. It means that the person you wish would ask you out is another guy on your baseball team.

But just because it is different doesn't mean it isn't the same in many ways. Lesbian and gay people fall in love just like anyone else does. They have the same thoughts and the same feelings—it's just that those feelings are for people of the same sex.

A lot of people think being lesbian or gay is all about sex. That's part of it. But it isn't the only part, just like being straight isn't only about having sex. A straight man may think a woman has a beautiful face, but he may be just as attracted to her kindness or her sense of humor. It's the same for a gay man. He may be attracted to another man's face, but he also enjoys the way that person laughs and carries himself. A straight woman may find a man's blue eyes sexually attractive, but she likes the way he listens to her even more. A lesbian may notice another woman's blue eyes, but also be drawn to her because they have great conversations.

Being a gay man means that there are things about men that you are drawn to, both sexually and emotionally. Being a lesbian means that you find women attractive for many different reasons. Lesbians and gay men love other women and men for the same reasons that straight men and women love one another. Some of those reasons are physical and sexual, but many more are emotional things that can't be easily explained.

There are several excellent books that answer basic questions about homosexuality, including:

Is It a Choice? (HarperCollins, 1993) by Eric Marcus. This easy-to-follow book provides answers to three hundred of the most frequently asked questions about lesbians and gays.

A Way of Love, A Way of Life: A Young Person's Introduction to What It Means to Be Gay (Lothrop, Lee & Shepard, 1979) by Frances Hanckel. One of the earliest books for young people about being gay, this book answers basic questions about homosexuality.

ALISON BECHDEL

CARTOONIST

For many people, reading comics is an important part of growing up. I know it was for me. I loved reading Green Lantern *and* Wonder Woman *comic books, as well as the Sunday comic strips. But there was always something missing from them—I never saw people who were like me, and I didn't know why.*

I wasn't the only kid who wondered where the gay people were. So did Alison Bechdel. Today, Alison is one of the most popular cartoonists in the gay community. Her nationally syndicated comic strip, "Dykes to Watch Out For," follows the ups and downs of a diverse group of women as they work, play, and love. It currently appears in more than fifty newspapers, and it has been collected in seven books.

A lot of gay people say that being a teenager was a horrible time in their lives. Did you have any negative experiences?
My life was okay until I hit junior high school, maybe around seventh grade. I guess I had sort of a sheltered life until I was twelve, because I went to

an alternative elementary school, where it was okay to be weird or different. But junior high was very stressful for me.

Why was that?
No one called me a "queer" or anything, but somehow I knew that I was one. I used a dictionary when I did my homework, and one of the guide words at the top of the page was *lesbian*. Whenever I had to look up something in the *L* section, I would flip through it really quickly, because I didn't want to see that word.

Was that because you knew it was what you were?
Not exactly. I didn't make the conscious connection, admitting it to myself, until I was nineteen. But I knew. You know how you know without having the words to describe it? I knew somehow that it was something I was trying to avoid.

But you felt different in some way?
I would get these little hints that I was gay. They weren't fully conscious. I remember the first time it really surfaced was one day in ninth grade. There was this girl that I had a crush on. I didn't really know that I had a crush on her. I just knew that I liked her, which to me is an interesting thing about growing up queer. You don't automatically have labels for your feelings like straight kids do. Even

though not having those easy definitions is bad in many ways, there is something I really treasure about that period of not knowing what was going on, because it was a way of having those feelings in their purest state, without having them packaged and commodified the way heterosexual feelings are. You know, straight sexuality is everywhere. It's shoved down everyone's throat from the time you're a little kid, and because of that, the innocence has been taken away from it. But when you're queer, and you don't have those labels or those expectations of what it's supposed to be like, you can experience it more fully.

So you had a crush on this girl and had all the butterflies and everything, but you didn't really know why?
Right. I was really into this girl. One day in English class, she fell—someone pushed her or something—and as she was getting up, she leaned back against my leg. It was like someone had branded me with a hot poker. In that one second, I knew that the feelings I was having were sexual—and I immediately thought that was wrong. So I spent the rest of my adolescence trying to bury it.

Did you just think those feelings were wrong, or had someone told you they were?
It wasn't so much that people around me talked

about homosexuality a lot. It was just assumed that
being queer was a bad, pathetic, nasty way to live
your life. You know, at that age everyone would call
one another "queer" as an epithet. It's just what kids
do. It wasn't so much that I had any particular message from my parents or the kids I hung out with. It
was just always in the background—something you
knew was strange, but you weren't sure why. There
was this overwhelming heterosexual message everywhere, and that was enough to make anything else
seem bad, because it wasn't what was being put forth
as "normal." You couldn't see queerness anywhere,
so the assumption was that it was wrong.

**When were you finally able to accept yourself and
come out?**
When I went to college. What enabled me to finally
do that, to kind of reconnect with this buried part
of myself, was partly the atmosphere I was in. I was
at a very progressive college, and although I didn't
know any gay men or lesbians at this point, I knew
that there were some around. The other part—the
more immediate part—was finding a book in the
campus bookstore of the documentary film *Word Is
Out*. The book was a transcription of the movie,
which was composed of interviews with real live gay
men and lesbians. I browsed through that book in
the store for a few days. I spent a lot of time in the
bookstore because I felt so lonely and out of it.

Then one day, standing there reading *Word Is Out,* I had this revelation. I hadn't really connected the book with my own life on a conscious level before, but all of a sudden, I *knew.* This fully formed realization came into my head that not only was I a lesbian but also that it was okay. Because I'd seen these people in this book, and they were all really cool. That seemed to make it okay for me to acknowledge that I was one, too, because now I knew that I could be one and be a regular person.

Did you ever buy the book?
Yes, I finally did. It took me awhile to get up my nerve, but I did it. By that point, I'd practically read the whole thing. But it was a wonderful moment, because for years and years I'd had this underlying feeling of not being like other people, of not being fully human. So to finally have a name for what I was gave me this great sense of realness. It was almost like being reborn.

Did you want to run out and tell everyone?
That's exactly what I did. I thought this was the greatest thing that had ever happened to me. All of a sudden, my whole life made sense. I spent months writing in my journal and fitting together this episode from my childhood and that feeling I'd had, and it was like putting a huge puzzle together. I was very happy about it. I didn't tell

everyone right away, but I gradually built up my confidence and came out to my roommate. And I went to this meeting for gay people on campus. And I wrote a letter to my parents.

But did you actually send it?
I did. And I didn't exactly get the positive response I'd expected. I don't know what I was thinking. You know, you're so idealistic when you're that age, and I'd just had this great moment of realization. I thought that they'd share in my jubilant self-discovery. But they were pretty wigged out by it. It sort of upset them. But they got over it.

How about your friends?
Well, I was in kind of a strange situation, because I had just transferred to this school, and I didn't know a lot of people. Most of the people I knew were straight guys. I told them, and they all tried to be really cool about it because they thought they should be. But gradually I shifted my focus to the queer people on campus. It was a mutual parting between me and my old friends.

How did you feel once you became part of a queer community?
It was strange at first. I wasn't used to being part of anything, so that was weird in itself. But I also wasn't used to thinking in any kind of a political

way, and the campus group I became a part of was very politicized. And that was hard for me. Being so public and making such a point out of being gay seemed strange.

Did it change you?
I very soon became one of those out, public people. I've never been a big activist or organizer or a community leader type. That's just not who I am. But I certainly came to understand the need to be public very early on. I knew it was important for people to know that we were out there.

What did you get out of being around other gay people?
It was like they saw my whole self. It was a way of being recognized completely for who I was. Plus, I was really hungry for hearing other people's stories. As far as I knew, for many, many years, I was the only one. And I'd had a lot of feelings and experiences that I thought no one else had ever had. Then I started learning that it wasn't just me, that there were a whole bunch of people who'd gone through this stuff, and that was very exciting. I felt that I was a real person in a way that I never had before. I'd always felt like I was some kind of alien, and now I was just a regular person.

Do you think straight people often assume that

everyone else has the same feelings they do?
In the straight world, the sexual level of people's lives is really a big deal—the way people flirt and date and form couples and all of that. But it was never anything I connected with or understood or could share with my straight friends. There was this way that I couldn't be as close to straight friends as I could to my new queer pals.

When did you start drawing the cartoon strip?
Well, I've always kind of been a cartoonist. I've always drawn funny pictures. My art teachers didn't think this was really art, but I did them at night in my notebooks. When I look back, I realize that the pieces I was doing for classes were really boring, but my own drawings had this spark to them. But the interesting thing is that I never drew women. All through my childhood and adolescence and college, I only drew men. After I came out as lesbian, it started to bug me that I was only drawing guys. So I tried to make myself draw women, and I couldn't do it with the same ease. What finally helped me learn to draw women was if I thought of the woman I was drawing as a lesbian. Then that connection was there, and I could draw her better than if I was just drawing a generic straight woman.

Do you think you avoided drawing women because you were afraid of being gay?

Learning to draw lesbians was my way of finally connecting with who I was. I started drawing these weird little pictures of lesbians in the margins of letters to friends, and I called them "Dykes to Watch Out For." I started numbering them—like "Dykes to Watch Out For, plate number 75," even though I'd only done three or four at that point. My friends liked them, and that inspired me to do more. Then I submitted them to a feminist newspaper I worked on—*Womanews*—and that's how it started.

Does a lot of the material come from your own life?

The early ones didn't. They were more surreal. To me, it was just exciting to see lesbians, to have pictures of people who were like me.

What do you find most rewarding about doing the strip?

There are a lot of things. First of all, it's a great job. I really, really love what I do. And I think that's so rare in our culture today. And I also love that my work has meaning to people, that people really follow this comic strip, and that it's a reflection of their lives that means something to them. Sometimes I think I would draw this strip even if no one else read it, because I am so hungry to see my life reflected, because I don't see it reflected in a genuine, realistic way anywhere else in this society. It's not portrayed in films or books or magazines. Or, if it is, it's presented in a bland, generic way. But I can write about these really particular, quirky facts of our subcultural queer life. And that's a really nourishing thing for me to do, and for people to see. Straight people see their lives reflected back at them a zillion times a day, and that's fine. But lesbians and gay men need to see their lives, too. The whole reason we create culture is because it's some kind of necessary affirmation to see yourself, to have a mirror. My strip is about the everyday life of a community of lesbians, and many different people can see their own lives there.

Are any of the characters you?
They are all a part of me. Each one represents something different. Sometimes people think I'm one or another—usually the character Mo—but all of them have a little bit of me. Mo is my anxious, conscientious side. Lois is my latent bad-girl side. Clarice is my workaholic side. They're all different aspects of my personality.

Do you ever feel like you might run out of ideas?
I used to. Before I used regular characters in my strip, I would just pick a topic each month and write about it. That was tough, because I started running out of topics. But now that I have my char-

acters, and their lives are set in motion, there's always something new happening. Friends fight and make up; the economy affects the feminist bookstore where Mo works; Clarice and Toni's baby is growing up; characters discuss current events. There's always something going on.

Do you draw from real-life issues in the queer community?

Sure. For example, Toni and Clarice are in the process of filing for second-parent adoption of their baby, Rafael. They want him to have two legal parents, instead of just Toni, the birth mother. It's a messy, complicated process that gay parents have to go through. I'm getting a lot of material from friends who've done it, so the strip is pretty true to life.

Looking back to when you were fifteen, could you ever have envisioned that your life would be like this?

Absolutely not. It's interesting, because I remember trying as a teenager to fantasize about my future. And a lot of that fantasy did look like my life does now. Like I have an art job and a really nice work space. I saw my work and my house very clearly. But I couldn't picture myself in a relationship. I knew that I wanted to be with someone, but when I tried to think of being with a man—which,

of course, was the only option I thought I had—I
just couldn't see anything. It was like looking in a
crystal ball and there was this mist over a big part
of it. And if you'd told me that I was going to be a
lesbian, I would have been horrified. I would have
pictured this sad, pathetic life living in bars or
something. I couldn't picture it any other way.

It's interesting to think about what my life would
have been like if I'd been able to see a positive
future earlier on. I see kids today who are twelve or
thirteen and who know that they're gay, and I
think how wonderful that must be. Because I never
had that. The really interesting thing will be when
little kids—if they happen to know when they're
five or six—start to be able to see these possibilities
for their lives. Imagine growing up seeing your life
as a gay person portrayed on TV like everyone
else's. I wonder what their lives will be like.

**Do you ever hear from young people who read
your work?**
Yes, more and more. I get a lot of letters from
young women whose mothers have my books. And
I actually get letters from nine-year-olds. One was
really funny. She said, "I'm a dyke," and she wanted
me to tell her how to be a dyke. I corresponded
with her for a while, though I explained to her that
there was no particular way to be a dyke.
Eventually, her mother enclosed a note saying how

glad she was that I was writing to her daughter. The mother was straight, but she had lesbian friends, and the little girl thought these women were just great, and she wanted to be like them.

Do you have any words of wisdom for young people reading this?
Oh, who am I to give advice? It's so hard when you're growing up and can't see a way out. I guess what I'd say is that whatever you're going through, it's always better when you grow up.

If you had told me when I was a kid that I was going to grow up to be a cartoonist who draws a lesbian comic strip, I wouldn't have believed you. I mean, the lesbian part was hard enough, but even the cartoonist part didn't seem very practical. My guidance counselor told me I should be a dental hygienist. But I did grow up to be a lesbian cartoonist, and if I can make a living drawing a comic strip called "Dykes to Watch Out For," anyone else can do anything they want to.

FUNNY STUFF

For a long time, the lives of gay people were not reflected in the pages of comic books or in the cartoons in newspapers and magazines. Now, however, many gay magazines and newspapers feature strips about lesbian and gay life, and even some of the big comic book publishers are beginning to feature gay characters.

If you are interested in comics with gay themes, you might want to check out these strips.

Alison Bechdel's comic strips have been collected in seven books: *Dykes to Watch Out For* (1986); *More Dykes to Watch Out For* (1988); *New, Improved! Dykes to Watch Out For* (1990); *Dykes to Watch Out For: The Sequel* (1992); *Spawn of Dykes to Watch Out For* (1993); *Unnatural Dykes to Watch Out For* (1995); and *Hot, Throbbing Dykes to Watch Out For* (1997). They can be found at lesbian and gay bookstores and women's bookstores, and are also available directly from the publisher, Firebrand Books.

Hothead Paisan by Diane DiMassa is a far-out strip available as a quarterly comic-zine. You can find it at lesbian and gay bookstores, as well as at some comic shops. The adventures of Hothead have also been collected in two books, both published by Cleis Press: *Hothead Paisan* (1993) and *The Revenge of Hothead Paisan* (1995).

Dyke Strippers: Lesbian Cartoonists from A to Z (Cleis Press, 1995), edited by Roz Warren, is a wonderful collection of work by many lesbian cartoonists.

For gay men, there are several comic strips that might be of interest. One of the oldest is "Wendel," written by Howard Cruse. The Wendel strips have been collected in the book *Wendel on the Rebound* (St. Martin's Press, 1989). Cruse is also the author of the critically acclaimed graphic novel *Stuck Rubber Baby* (Harper Perennial, 1995), which is the story of his life as a gay man.

Another very popular gay comic strip that has been collected in book form is Eric Orner's *The Mostly Unfabulous Social Life of Ethan Green* (St. Martin's Press, 1992). The strip also appears in numerous gay magazines and papers. Further misadventures of Ethan Green are collected in *The 7 Deadly Sins of Love* (St. Martin's Press, 1994) and *The Ethan Green Chronicles* (St. Martin's Press, 1997).

LESBIAN AND GAY FAST FACT TWO

Why Are Some People Gay or Lesbian?

If you ask a straight person why she or he is straight, you will probably get a really funny look in return. To them, it seems like a ridiculous question. Yet straight people will frequently ask lesbian and gay people why they are gay. They don't think this is a strange question at all. This is because in our society, most people are straight, so everyone grows up surrounded by images of what it means to be a straight person. We're taught that women and men date and get married and have children. That's just the way it is. People who are straight don't really have to think about *why* they are the way they are, because everyone else seems to be doing things the same way.

But lesbian and gay people aren't doing things the same way everyone else is, and many people want to know why. Why don't gay people act just like everyone else? Why do some people feel attracted to people of the same sex? Why can't gay people "change" and be straight?

The answer is that no one really knows why some people are gay and some aren't. There are lots of theories as to why, but that is all they are—theories. There are no proven facts behind them. Some people used to think that boys would become gay if they didn't play sports, or that girls would turn into lesbians if they did. Others believed that girls who spent too much time with their fathers would be lesbians, and that boys whose mothers spoiled them would be gay. Today we realize those ideas are foolish, but for many years people thought they were proof of why some people were gay.

More recently, some people have suggested that there is a "gay gene" that makes people gay, the same way genes make some people redheaded or left-handed. Maybe this is true; maybe it isn't.

It is human nature to want to know why people are different, because once we know the reason, we feel more comfortable around them. And if we happen to be one of those people others are trying to figure out, knowing why we are different can make us feel less different.

But ultimately, it doesn't matter why any of us are gay or straight, because it isn't going to change anything. What's important is that we stop worrying about why some people are different and start understanding that each of us is a person who deserves respect. When we start to do that, then all of these labels that we give one another won't mean anything.

Obviously, it's easier to say that than actually to do it. But it isn't impossible. If you are a lesbian or gay person, try not to worry so much about why you are different. Instead, concentrate on all of the qualities you have that make you who you are. There are a lot of them, and each one is special. Being gay is just another special part of who you are.

If you aren't gay, it may be hard for you to understand people who are. You may think they're weird or strange. You may even be afraid of them. Those feelings are okay, but try to think about *why* you believe gay people are strange or frightening. Also think about what it would be like to be different from most of the people around you, and how that would make you feel. Once you start to do this, you may find that your feelings about gay people begin to change.

As for the idea of gay people "changing" and becoming straight, that isn't very realistic. For many years, homosexuality was considered by some people to be a form of mental illness that could be "cured" by various therapies, some of which were harmful or even deadly. But the more doctors and therapists learned about gay people, the more they understood that homosexuality is not an illness. And in 1973, the American Psychiatric Association officially removed homosexuality from its list of personality disorders.

This did not stop some people from still seeking cures, however, and many lesbian and gay people went or were sent to therapists and doctors in attempts to make them straight. This was particularly true, and is still sometimes true, of gay young people, many of whom were taken to doctors by their parents, who had no idea of what else to do. Often, the people looking to be cured of their homosexuality were extremely unhappy with their lives for many reasons and were seeking ways to feel more accepted by their families or by society. Unfortunately, the therapies used to try to help them often did more harm than good.

Today, most therapists believe that showing patients how to accept themselves for who they are is a much more realistic and healthy approach to dealing with a person's concerns about her or his sexuality.

There are, however, groups that claim to "reform" homosexuals and make them straight. These groups are generally religious in nature, and their members are subjected to very strict supervision. While some people who have undergone the programs say that they have changed their sexual orientation because of these groups, many more have spoken out against their tactics and teachings.

MARK LEDUC

OLYMPIC SILVER MEDALIST IN BOXING

When I was growing up, I used to watch the Olympic Games on television. I was always amazed at how strong the divers were, how fast the runners were, and how graceful the skaters were. But I could never imagine myself doing any of those things, because I didn't think gay people could. I had this idea that they just weren't cut out for sports.

When I became involved in the gay community, I discovered that this wasn't true. I found that a lot of people I met had been active in sports all their lives. In fact, I learned that some of the Olympic athletes I'd admired so much were gay, too. I wished I had known that when I was watching them dive and swim and run, because it would have made me feel proud to be a gay person myself.

Today, there are some out gay athletes. One of them is Mark Leduc. A member of the Canadian boxing team, Mark won a Silver Medal at the 1986 Olympic Games in Barcelona, Spain. After turning professional, he became the Canadian superlightweight champion. He was a Canadian sports hero, and he is very much admired by his fans and the sports community. While Mark had

*always been out about his sexuality and his relationship
with his lover, he came out publicly in 1994 on a television documentary called* For the Love of the Game.
*Mark is now retired from boxing. A sports-program
administrator, he spends a lot of his time volunteering for
gay and AIDS groups in Toronto, where he lives.*

**Did you know that you were gay when you were
young?**
I knew that I was gay at a fairly young age. At
least, I knew that I was attracted to men. I kind of
accepted it as I was approaching adolescence. But
I don't think I knew what that meant for my life.

**That was also around the time that you began to
box. Do you think you chose boxing—which is
seen as being very masculine—as a way maybe to
not be gay?**
I'm not sure. I don't think so, but at some level it
may have been. I was always a natural athlete, but I
didn't like team sports. Boxing was good for me
because how well I did depended on how much
work I put into it. It was just me, not a whole team.

I think my sport actually helped me deal with
those feelings. By submerging myself in boxing, I
learned to be more comfortable with being
myself—part of which meant being gay—and with
being a man in general. I also liked all the attention I got at that young age. I don't think young

people get the attention they need from adults. They're ignored and pushed aside a lot. So by being noticed at a young age, I felt that I was really good at something, which made me feel good about who I was as a person.

Did you know anything about gay people when you first realized you were attracted to men?
No. I had no idea, and I did not have very good conceptions as I got older. I was told that they were perverted, that they dressed in women's clothing—all those derogatory kinds of things.

But you never applied them to yourself?
No, because I'd been brought up well by my parents. I liked who I was, the person I was, regardless of whether I was gay or not. And I was honest with myself. I knew I wasn't bad or anything like that. Things like that helped me develop more as a person, rather than just as a gay person. Even though I was gay, I sort of put it on a back burner and ignored it for a while and I worked on just being an all-around person. Maybe because I wasn't what people perceived as a stereotypical gay person, it never really came up. I was like any other kid—a little mischievous, running all over the place exploring. I had a few friends, but we never really talked about girls or anything at that age, so it didn't come up.

And you never had the perception that you couldn't be in sports, especially something macho like boxing, because you were gay?
I started at such a young age that I didn't even know what my sexuality was, so it didn't occur to me. I knew I liked men. I knew I'd rather talk to men than to women, and I confided in men much more than in women. But these are things I see looking back now. I didn't understand then what it might mean. You know, I never questioned why it was I would rather have a man comfort me than a woman.

How did things change as you got older?
Eventually, I made it onto the national boxing team. Because I was the oldest team member, I sort of set the example for the rest of the guys. I didn't smoke or drink or chase girls. A lot of the guys on those teams are pretty young, and they forget why they are going out there, why our government is putting all this money into them, which is to produce medals for the country.

What about your sexuality? Was it an issue?
I didn't really speak openly about it. But after four years of traveling together, you get to know one another rather well. People pretty much knew. They knew my boyfriend. They knew I'd phone him and write to him. They'd be writing their girl-friends or calling them, and I'd be calling him. But

they never bothered me about it. Each member of the team really earned his right to be there. We'd each won our respective weight divisions, and we each had the drive and desire to achieve that. So, sure, they'd try and pick on someone when they found a weakness in him, but there was also this respect we had for one another because we all knew what it took to get where we were. And I didn't tolerate anyone saying anything derogatory, about gay people or anything else. So people knew that if they said anything out of line, I'd take them on, either verbally or physically if I had to. Not in a bullying way, but in a decent way. I'm not a tough guy in a stereotypical way. I'm really fairly quiet and conservative. I don't pick fights to prove anything.

Did you ever feel you had to work harder than other boxers to be accepted, or did you have trouble from guys on other teams?
Once I turned pro, they knew I was gay. And that's when I ran into a lot of difficulty. The managers and promoters in the pro business were very, very homophobic. And I felt that some of the boxers felt it was their duty to try and beat the queer.

What about during the Olympics?
The Olympics were great. There were rumors, of course, because I didn't hide. I'd go out with my

boyfriend and hold his hand, and people would see that. People see things like that and talk. I remember one time word had been going around, and one of the national coaches came up to me prior to the games in Barcelona. He said, "You know, I heard this rumor that you're gay." And I said, "Would that make me a bad person, or a bad guy? Does that mean you'd have to watch me in the showers or something?" I was very up front, because I've never had anything to hide and never will. And he didn't really say anything. I was disappointed in him, because he wouldn't really talk about it honestly. I sort of felt that he was using this as a way to get at me.

How did it feel winning at the Olympics and standing on the medal platform as a gay man and the number two boxer in the world?
To me it didn't feel like "Here's one for the good guys" or anything. There was nothing political about it for me. I was most proud of being as honest as I could be, and I knew it was only by the grace of God that I'd accomplished my goals. It was a personal sense of thanks that I'd been able to overcome many things in my life to become this athlete who was standing there. That's something I am very thankful for. I'm thankful that I am able to be open and honest, and that I have love in my life.

Why did you come out so publicly on national television?

I find it really irritating when people try to exploit me by threatening my sexuality or trying to use it against me. That's one of the reasons I officially came out on national television. I wanted to make it very clear who I am and what I'm about, without rumors. People get really odd ideas, like assuming that because you're gay, you're after their children or something. They can't digest the fact that yes, I may teach children and have involvement with them, but I'm not at all a child molester or a pervert or anything. It really hurts me when those types of ideas are in people's minds, because they're so false. I think the media has a lot to do with it. All the stereotypes people have of gay men come from what they see. You know, gay men like men, not little boys.

Did you have problems with people thinking those things about you?

At the time I came out, I had opened a gym, and I did teach a lot of kids. And again, there were rumors going around about me, so I knew that coming out would put an end to them. It puts people in their place, because it takes away their power to hurt you. When you come out and say, "This is who I am," they can't hurt you. I knew a lot of men who had young boys whom I looked after at the gym, and they said, "I trust Mark with my son because he's a good guy." And things like that make you feel really good. We still have a long way to go, but it's a start.

Why don't you think more sports figures come out?
It's hard to understand unless you're involved in it. When you're competing in a sport, your entire mind is trained on that sport. Forget the obstacles associated with coming out. You're just totally focused on training. So it isn't always that people are unwilling to come out; it's just that it's not something they have time to think about. If you are an athlete in an individual sport, like I was, sometimes the battle over your being gay ends up being worked out one-on-one when you fight someone. And if you're involved in a team sport, it's all about the team, not about you. And then you have things to worry about, like dealing with how guys in a locker room will react if you come out. There are many little things to think about.

It is unfortunate that gay athletes can't always set the examples they need to set or should set. But there is so much that gets in the way. I think people forget that because they're so anxious to have role models.

What happened when you came out?
There were no real problems. There was a change

in the camaraderie of the other athletes. People weren't so quick maybe to hang out with me or be friends with me. I didn't compete anymore after that. I still get a lot of people, including young people, coming up and saying, "We wish you'd come back." But it's not what I want to do.

Do you find being part of the gay community has been a positive part of your life?
Yes. But I think the gay community can also be something of an illusion, especially to young people. I think there are many issues that gay people, especially gay men, have not dealt with yet. And for young people, the idea of being let loose in the gay community can be very appealing, when really it can be very dangerous if you aren't ready. Many gay people have problems with self-esteem, which can lead to problems with alcohol or drug use because they have never been able to address their problems and are running from who they are.

Do you see a lot of gay young people?
I speak a lot to gay youth. I see them out and about, and I talk to them. I try to set a good example for them. A lot of people recognize me, so I try to be able to give good advice.

Is it hard to be just Mark and not Mark the gay boxer?

I think it's harder for everyone else. I think people expect me to be outspoken, violent, aggressive, or something. But I'm not. And I'm not impressed by people who are. I'm really trying to stay away from sports-oriented things. I had my day, and I'm more than just an athlete. I'm more than just a boxer and more than just a gay man. I want to put my energy where I feel it's needed.

You've done a lot of work with AIDS organizations. Is that something that's important to you?

I'm really happy to be part of the gay community at the time we're in now. HIV and AIDS have devastated us, and I think it's remarkable how even in this time of trouble we still shine brighter than we ever have before. I think we've become pioneers in the gay movement because of how we have dealt with the AIDS crisis. It's brought us closer. Some people may never, ever understand what it's done, but out of the bad has come a lot of good. For the first time really we've banded together to fight socially, economically, and politically over a common cause.

Do you think it's sometimes hard for gay young people to think that they're worth worrying about?

Gay young people do have a lot to deal with. There are many messages they get from their parents and their friends and from the media, and all of these things can be overwhelming. It's killing many of them. Many gay kids still kill themselves. And we need to start showing kids that there are options.

Self-image is so important, and sometimes so hard to have. You have to look at yourself and be able to say, "I'm not a nerd. I'm not a freak," which is what so many gay kids think of themselves. People want to be part of the cool crowd. But if you look at the cool crowd, they really aren't so great. They're really pretty shallow and thoughtless and careless. Instead of worrying about what people think, you're better off developing your mind and getting to know yourself.

You know, I'm very traditional. I believe in family and all of that, and I think the best thing is to have one partner. Now obviously, not everyone believes this, but I think it's what's best for me. I really believe that if you get to know yourself, then some-day you'll meet that person who is your soul mate. And I think I was able to do that because I spent so much time getting to know myself.

What's been the most important thing you've learned from your experiences?
I think the most important thing was developing the faith to say, "Okay, I screwed up a lot as a youth. Now I'm going to be who I am and what I am. And this is what I am—I am a gay male. And by loving another gay male, there's nothing wrong with me.

I'm going to be as honest as I can with myself, and with everyone. I'm going to do what I do best and do it as well as I can. Of course, I had a great training program and coaches and teachers. But in the end, it all comes down to yourself. You establish your own self-worth and value in life. And I put my trust in believing that what I'm doing is the right thing. And by doing that, everything fell together for me. I've been very, very lucky. It's been fortunate how life has evolved the way it has.

You know, sometimes you get to a point in your life where you look at what you've done. And maybe you've screwed up a lot, and maybe a lot of that has to do with your struggle to accept being gay. But you accept that, and you move on, and you say you're not afraid and nothing will stop you. When you can do that, no one can stop you.

Do you think having gay role models can really help you do that?
I didn't have a lot of gay role models, or any role models, but I had decent men and women who set examples for me to follow and live up to. And that's what you need. You can't be just like someone else, and you shouldn't be. Everyone is different. But it's great to have people who inspire you in different ways.

Does it make you feel good knowing that maybe you're that person for other people?

If someone can maintain his kindness and tough-ness and respect, then I'm proud to have him look up to me. I think it's wonderful that we live in a time when a kid can be a so-called faggot and be the toughest kid on the block. Not that I condone violence. I don't believe being tough is what makes you a man. It's just one part of what a man is, or what a man is perceived as. I think what's most important is being perceived as decent and honest. You are a man regardless of what you are. Some people see a man as someone who is tough and strong and who can split firewood and fix cars and sleep with twenty women a night. There are so many confusing ideas about what being a man is, and as a young person, it's easy to be confused or to give in to peer pressure to act certain ways. But we all need to find our own perspectives and what we need out of life.

How can gay kids—who might be surrounded by negative images of gay people—do that?

I think what gay kids need to do is accept their sex-uality as part of who they are and move on. Don't let other people's ideas or perceptions cripple your potential. Look at what's in front of you. So many people cripple themselves with fear of being gay. They pass up goals and opportunities because they're so afraid. Fear is your best friend. Fight and learn from it.

A lot of people feel that if they aren't liked or loved—or if they think that God doesn't love them—then there's no use living. And that's a lie. What people tell you and what you feel in your heart are two different things. Listen to what you believe about yourself, not what other people say about you. I know there are people who don't like me, and I don't care. I really don't. People who do know me, who know what I really am, accept me. And there's nothing you can do about what the other people think.

TIME OUT! GAYS AND LESBIANS AND SPORTS

There are many groups that offer sports activities for lesbians and gay men. There are gay running groups, gay softball leagues, gay hiking and camping groups, gay tennis leagues, and even a gay rodeo association. Once every four years, the gay community also holds the Gay Games, an event like the Olympic Games, where lesbian and gay people compete in various activities, from wrestling and volleyball to figure skating and weight lifting. The best way to find out about gay athletic groups in your area is to pick up a copy of the local gay newspaper, which usually will contain listings for such things.

If you're interested in finding out more about lesbians and gay men in sports, here are some books you might find interesting.

Behind the Mask: My Double Life in Baseball (Viking, 1990) by Dave Pallone, with Alan Steinberg. Pallone was a successful major-league baseball umpire, until he came out of the closet and was forced out of the game.

Breaking the Surface: A Life (Random House, 1995) by Greg Louganis, with Eric Marcus. Louganis is probably the most popular diver ever to compete in the sport. A multiple Gold Medal winner in both the 1984 and 1988 Olympic Games, he is also HIV-positive. This is his story.

Icebreaker: The Autobiography of Rudy Galindo (Pocket Books, 1997) by Rudy Galindo, with Eric Marcus. The life story of the first openly gay figure skater and winner of the 1996 men's title at the US National Figure Skating Championships.

Lesbians and Gays and Sports (Chelsea House, 1994) by Perry Deane Young. A history of gay people in the sports world, written for young people.

Martina: The Lives and Times of Martina Navratilova (Birch Lane Press, 1995) by Adrianne Blue. Navratilova, who is one of the gay community's most visible spokespeople, is also considered the greatest women's tennis player in the history of the game.

Sportsdykes: Stories from On and Off the Field (St. Martin's Press, 1995), edited by Susan Fox Rogers. This is a collection of writings by lesbians about the sports they love to play.

LESBIAN AND GAY FAST FACT **THREE**

How Many Gay People Are There?

At one time or another, just about every gay person has thought that she or he was the only one around. And many straight people think they don't know any gay people. For some people, this may be true, but it's doubtful. Gay people are everywhere.

No one knows exactly how many gay people there are in the world. Because they look just like anyone else, you can't really go out and count them. Various estimates have suggested that gay people make up as little as 2 percent of the total population; others put the numbers as high as 20 percent. In reality, there's no way to know for sure how many gay people there are, but it is generally believed that they make up about 10 percent of the population—meaning that one out of every ten people is gay.

This may not seem like a lot of people, but compare it to some other groups. According to the United States Census Bureau's 1997 estimates,

African American people make up a little less than 13 percent of the population in the United States. Asian people make up about 4 percent. That means that there are almost as many gay people as there are African Americans, and more than twice as many gay people as there are Asian Americans. When you think about it that way, you see that represents a lot of people.

What makes it seem as if there aren't many lesbian and gay people is that we are invisible. By that I mean that you generally can't tell people are gay just by looking at them. You can see how many African American people there are in our communities because the color of their skin makes them visible. The same with Caucasian people or Hispanic or Asian. Each of these groups has a distinct appearance, making them easy to see. But gay people come from all of these different groups, and we aren't always immediately visible. This makes it difficult for people to really understand how many of us there are.

To get an idea of how many gay people may be living around you, think about that 10 percent figure. If there are two hundred people in your school, chances are about twenty of them are gay or lesbian. If there are three thousand people in your town, three hundred might be gay. Obviously, this isn't always going to be true. Sometimes there will be more gay people; sometimes there will be fewer. Sometimes where you live will affect how many gay people live there. In New York City, for example, there will be a higher percentage of gay people than in a small town in West Virginia. But wherever you live, you can be pretty sure there are gay people.

Now, knowing that there *might* be other gay and lesbian people around isn't the same as actually knowing any. But sometimes just knowing there are other people like you can keep you going.

NANCY GARDEN
WRITER

When I was growing up, I searched the library for books about lesbian and gay people. I found very few, and none that showed gay people as being happy. Then I discovered Nancy Garden's book Annie on My Mind. *Published in 1982, the book is the story of Liza and Annie, two girls who fall in love and have to deal with the pressures brought about by their own feelings and the feelings of the people around them. It was the first time I'd ever read that gay and lesbian people could have happy lives filled with love and laughter. Many people I know—especially lesbians—said the same thing about the book.*

In 1993, Annie on My Mind *came under attack by religious groups in and around Kansas City, Kansas, and Kansas City, Missouri. A group called Project 21, whose purpose is to encourage schools to include fair, accurate information about gays and lesbians in their libraries and curricula, had donated Nancy Garden's book, along with* All-American Boys *by Frank Mosca, to forty-two schools in the Kansas City area. When several people complained, a firestorm of controversy erupted. A fundamentalist minister burned* Annie *in front of the*

building housing the board of education, and a few
school officials, discovering that copies of Annie on My
Mind *had been on their library shelves for years, ordered*
the book removed.

Students and librarians protested. There were angry
meetings and letters to the editor, and Nancy Garden
went to Kansas City at the invitation of the local
Coalition Against Censorship to speak about the ban-
ning. When officials refused to restore the book to school
library shelves, a group of students and parents in
Olathe, Kansas, sued in federal district court. After a
trial at which they, local librarians, and Garden testified,
the book was returned to circulation. The battle was won,
thanks to all those people who stood up to the censors.

You've written more than twenty books, mainly for
young adults. Was having children something you
wanted?
One of the first questions a straight friend asked
when I came out to her was, "But won't you miss
having children?" And my response was, "Well, yes,
but that's not all there is to life." I really thought it
was not an option for me, even adoption. But one
of the most rewarding relationships in my life has
been with a young woman whom my partner,
Sandy, and I kind of nurtured, especially between
the time she was twelve and when she went off to
college. She was a neighbor from a dysfunctional
family, and she and her twin brother spent many,

many hours with us. We sort of felt that they were our kids in a way. Of course, we didn't have a lot of the usual parental responsibilities, but we often knew more about what was going on with these kids than their parents did.

Did the parents acknowledge this?
Oh, yes. They—especially the mother—were very grateful for it. It was nice that they allowed the kids to know us. We are still very much in contact with the girl, and sometimes with her brother, as well.

What was it like for you growing up?
It was very tough. I didn't know specifically about myself. I felt different, without knowing why. I spent a lot of time wanting to be a boy, and pretending I was. One of my favorite Christmas presents was a pair of dungarees. And I very distinctly remember one day being a real tomboy in the morning, wearing dungarees and climbing trees and stuff, and then in the afternoon putting on a skirt and trying to be ladylike and take care of a doll. It was as though I was experimenting, even though I wasn't conscious of that. I used to hate it when my father opened a door for me. I wanted to say, "Hey, I'm strong enough to do that myself." I was never very athletic, but I remember once having a roller-skating race with a boy and beating him. He was furious and I was proud.

Did you want to be a boy?
I did. You know, for a long time people thought that all gay people wanted to be the opposite sex, which obviously isn't true. But for many years, I thought I wanted to be a boy. It took me a long time to accept that I was female and to be happy with that.

Were your parents encouraging of this?
Sort of. My mother was a very strong woman. She grew up on a chicken farm. And my father always sent mixed signals. He told me that girls could do anything boys could do, but that they'd have to do it better because boys didn't agree. That was a great message, and he was proud of me in many ways. But he was also very upset that I wasn't terribly feminine. He wanted me to wear pink dresses and frills and that sort of thing. Especially when I was in my teens and my twenties, I was pretty butch, so I was not his image of a great daughter. I think that when it got toughest was in high school, which is true for most gay people. That's when I fell in love with Sandy, which was wonderful but also very difficult.

So you met Sandy in school. That's very much like the plot of *Annie on My Mind*. Is the book your story?
Not really, but in some ways it is based on what happened to us. We were in a private all-girls school.

She was a class ahead of me. We first met when we were twelve, but we didn't really get to know each other until we were sixteen, when we were in a group of one-act plays at the boys school affiliated with our school. She was in one play and I was in another. We got to talking at rehearsals, and we found out we had a lot in common. We became very close very quickly, and it was very romantic. We each knew what the other was thinking, we used to pass notes to each other in school between classes, and we spent every moment we could together. Then her mother found a letter I had written her. I don't remember what it said, but something in it suggested to her that I was a lesbian.

Did she tell Sandy she thought you were gay?
She did. I don't think I had ever even heard the word before. I didn't know what it was. But when I found out, it all started to make a great deal of sense. I remember finding an article about gay men in the magazine section of the Sunday paper. I read it, and it made sense to me. Anyway, eventually Sandy's parents said they wouldn't allow her to see me outside of school. But she did.

Did they tell your parents?
Yes. My father was away a lot at that point, so he didn't really know what was going on. My mother didn't agree. She wrote a letter back to Sandy's

mother saying that it was foolish to keep us apart.

But did she agree that you were a lesbian?
You know, I don't know if she did or not. I think she would have accepted it, but she never really knew. I did eventually date boys, and in college I convinced myself I was in love with a boy. My mother died around that time, and we never talked about my being gay. But I know she would have accepted it. She was a social worker, and a very loving, wonderful person. We were very close. My father would not have accepted it then, and I think he was never really reconciled to it, but that's a later part of the story. While we were still in high school, Sandy and I went on seeing each other, and we got caught. And we did it again and got caught. Things went on like that for a long time.

Did you and Sandy discuss being lesbians?
Endlessly. We discussed it. We denied it. We would act on it and then say it wasn't true. I was a little calmer about it than Sandy was. My main feeling was that I wanted to know. I wanted a message to be handed to me, saying, "This is what you are." I wanted to know this for absolute sure. That was really my main hang-up, along with the upheaval caused by her parents, who eventually told her that if we were caught together again, they would not allow her to go to college, and that she'd have to

go to secretarial school. Sandy was—is—very bright, so this was an awful thing to have hanging over her. Eventually, she went to the headmistress of our school and told her, and the woman very kindly said not to worry about it, that the school would make sure she got to college. So she had at least that assurance. But it didn't make things much easier. It was a very dramatic time. For example, I remember on several occasions being in a car with Sandy and seeing one of her parents and then ducking down under the dashboard. We had to be very secretive.

Were there times when you thought it was too much?
I remember one day driving with Sandy down a road that ended in a stone wall, and for a moment I thought—as a lot of gay kids do, I think—that I just wouldn't stop. I thought that if we died, at least we'd be together and all the pain would be over. But obviously I didn't do that.

What eventually happened with you two?
Sandy graduated and went off to college, and I was left to finish my senior year. She wrote to me, and she came home for vacation, but soon after Thanksgiving or Christmas she decided that it was all too hard. She said we'd have to break it off, but she also said that if I ever needed her, I should just

call. That got me through many hard times. I was in theater in those days, and in my first season of summer stock, between my junior and senior years in high school, I met a gay guy. He and I stayed up all one night sharing our experiences, and that was wonderful. But other than that, I didn't have any support from other gay people.

That must have been awful.
It was. Sandy and I had looked for information, of course. We looked in encyclopedias, but in that era there was nothing. If there was, it said you were sick, paranoid, schizophrenic. Obviously, according to encyclopedias, you were doomed. I looked for fiction, but that wasn't very helpful, either. When I found books listed under *homosexuality* in the library's card catalog, they were never in. At the time, I didn't realize that was deliberate. Someone was keeping the books off the shelves on purpose, which, of course, is an act of censorship. Down at the local bus station, I found some paperback books with lurid covers that were supposedly about lesbians. But they all ended in suicide, mental illness, or in a guy coming along and snatching up the young lesbian and riding off into the sunset to make her all better. The only helpful book I found was Radclyffe Hall's *The Well of Loneliness,* which is the book most lesbians my age discovered. [*The Well of Loneliness* is a 1928 novel about a les-

bian named Stephen Gordon and her battle to live life freely as a lesbian.]

That book is so depressing, though, because nothing goes right for the main character. But did it help?
It did. It became my bible. I read it and reread it over and over again. And I vowed at that point that I was going to write a gay book that ended happily, a book about my people.

Were you writing then?
I was writing a lot of agonized poetry—very melodramatic. It was me on a soapbox, saying, "You must understand us!" I also wrote plays, but they were all conversations that Sandy and I'd actually had. They were very earnest, although pretty awful.

How about your friend from summer stock? Did you continue to be friends?
Yes, we still are friends. He taught me gay vocabulary, which I didn't know at all. During my senior year, when our school held dances and we were all expected to invite boys, he would go with me. For a while, I'd dated a cast-off boyfriend of Sandy's. She had been forced to date by her parents, and she did a lot more of that than I did. But I went out with one of her old boyfriends, and I remember his kissing me and my wishing he would just go away. I

hated it. And I even remember saying to my mother, "It's so different when John kisses me from when Sandy kisses me." But when my gay friend and I went to school dances, it was fun, because here we were, two gay people pretending to be straight and fooling everyone. We had a good time.

Did either of you know any other gay people?
He knew more people, but I didn't. I had my suspicions about some of the other students in school, and about some of the teachers, as well. But I didn't know for sure. It turned out that I was right, at least in a couple of cases, but I didn't know it then.

At some point when I was in college, my gay friend and I decided to become engaged, because it seemed like a good solution. But I told him that if Sandy and I ever got back together, it would be over. In the end, we never got married. I balked at announcing it to our families. My mother was pretty skeptical about it all anyway. But it gave us a certain status, and that was nice.

There were some other dykes at college—I went to Columbia University's School of Dramatic Arts—but we were never entirely sure about one another. So I didn't really have a circle of gay friends.

How did you and Sandy get back together?
I continued to do summer stock, and one of my jobs was lighting design. And one night while I was

hanging lights, I fell eighteen feet onto a concrete floor. I broke my back. I wanted to get in touch with Sandy at that point, but I didn't. Then one of our neighbors back home told her, and she wrote me a letter. Hearing from her was wonderful. Six or eight months later, though, when my mother was dying, I did call Sandy, and she came to be with me. She was about to graduate from college, and she had a job in New York, where I was living. So we got back together again. Then we broke up, but later we got back together again for good. We've been together ever since.

Did Sandy tell her mother that the two of you were back together?
I think her sister did. And I know her mother cried about it. But her mother has sort of come to acknowledge me after all these years. She's outwardly accepting—as many people are—even though she doesn't like it.

What did your father say?
I didn't tell him until *Annie* came out.

Let's talk about that. You said earlier that you were determined to write a book about gay people. How did you start writing for young people?
I always liked writing. When I was little, I used to write for fun. I loved books and reading, and I

loved children's books. Even when I grew up, I loved them, and I've always loved children. Writing for them seemed like a natural thing to do. I also wanted to write adult books, and in college I drafted a novel called *For Us Also,* which was something of a cross between Radclyffe Hall and the Bible, so it's a good thing it never got published. But it was a very therapeutic thing to do, and I learned a lot from it. Then when I was getting over my back accident, I read a lot and wrote some things.

Did you read any of the early gay young adult books like Isabelle Holland's *The Man Without a Face* and John Donovan's *I'll Get There; It Better Be Worth the Trip?*
Oh, sure; I seized upon them. And a lot of that early stuff, like Donovan's book, really made me feel that maybe I could write about it too.

How did you get started?
I sent manuscripts to magazines. I sold only one story and one poem. This was discouraging to me. But then, through a series of coincidences, I got an agent and started getting work. I wrote several novels and nonfiction books before I decided to try addressing the gay issue. Then I wrote a book called *Summerhut,* but this book was still me standing on my soapbox. One of the hardest things for a young writer to realize is that often the thing

that's closest to you is the thing that's hardest to write about. And the hardest lesson to learn is how to tell a story when you have a political point to make. I hadn't quite learned that yet. When I sent *Summerhut* out, it didn't sell.

Sometime later, I drafted another gay book called *Good Moon Rising*, which had a theater setting. I had left theater long before that, but it had been like a god to me—my religion almost. I felt so emotional about having left it that it was almost impossible for me to go into a theater. Writing *Good Moon Rising*—which on the one hand was gay and on the other was about theater—was a real catharsis for me. I thought it wasn't any good, though, and put it away. I got it out again a couple of years ago, worked on it more, and it was published. But back in the 1970s, when I'd abandoned *Good Moon Rising*, I was still determined to write a gay book for kids. One rainy day—I remember I was eating tomato soup for lunch—the line "It's raining, Annie" popped into my head. I went upstairs and started writing, and that was the beginning of *Annie on My Mind*, which became my tenth published book.

Did you have trouble selling it because it was about gay young people?
Much to my surprise, I didn't. Farrar, Straus & Giroux had published one of my other books. When

my editor there read the manuscript, she loved it and urged the house to publish it. And they did.

Were you apprehensive about its coming out?
I was, because of my family and because Sandy and I had moved to a small town and knew a lot of people there. We were very active in town government, and I was afraid of what people might think. I told my favorite aunt, with whom I'm very close, about it and she was fine. She hadn't seemed fine about gay people in general when I was younger, but we had become good friends over the years. When I told her about it, and that I was gay, she reminded me of two elderly women she and my mother had grown up knowing, who were referred to as "The Aunts." They weren't really aunts, but they were friends of the family. They were clearly lesbians, and my aunt said, "Well, look at The Aunts. There have always been people like this." She's been very supportive and loving all along.

What was your father's reaction when you told him that you were gay?
His reaction was, "What did I do wrong?" He was also disappointed because he had always wanted grandchildren, desperately, and now he wasn't going to have any. But he knew Sandy and he loved her, and I think that helped him adjust. He had to reconcile his feelings of disappointment with his fondness for

Sandy. Still, after that time, we almost never talked about it. I would sometimes force the issue, but he was very uncomfortable with it. For a long time, *Annie* did not appear on his bookshelf with all my other books. And then one day, it appeared, but it would disappear every now and then, maybe depending on who was coming to visit or as he dealt with my being gay in different degrees.

Were you afraid for your career as a children's book writer at all?
A little. I was nervous about it. But I reminded myself that writing this book was something I'd always wanted to do. It was something I'd vowed to do and was committed to. I didn't like hiding; I didn't want to hide anymore. And, in fact, there really wasn't any flack when it came out.

What was it like holding it when you got your copies?
It was like holding my very first book. It was marvelous. I felt it was the most important book that I had ever written. It certainly was the one I loved the most.

Is it still?
I think so. It's hard to say. Many writers say that the book you're working on at the moment is the most important to you, and I think on the whole they're

right. There are others that I like very much, but I think *Annie's* still my favorite in many ways. And I'm still always amazed and touched when new people discover it and write to me.

Were you surprised at the positive impact it had?

In one way, I wasn't, because I knew people needed it. As I said earlier, I'd looked for a book like it when I was growing up, and the letters I got confirmed that a lot of other people did, too. That was extremely gratifying. One of the best responses came from a teenage girl whose mother was a newspaper reporter. Her mother had asked her to read the book, because she was reviewing it and wanted to see what an average teenager thought of it. The girl didn't want to read it because it was about "those people." But she did, and when she was done, she said, "Those girls are just like any other girls falling in love." And that was great, because that's exactly what I wanted to say in the book.

Was there any negative reaction?

The thing I remember most is a hate letter I got from a woman who wanted the book removed from her local library. She thought that it was evil and that I was evil, and she quoted Scripture, implying I should be drowned. I kept that letter on my desk for about three weeks, trying to figure out what to say to her. Ultimately, I didn't answer her.

Then in 1993, the book was actually burned in Kansas City. Right before it happened, I had told a group I was speaking to that *Annie* had never had much trouble. Then I got home and received this phone call saying the book had been burned. It was a total shock. I didn't know how to respond. I had this mental picture of the book burning, and it was just horrible.

What were you most surprised at about the censorship?

That there are many, many wonderful people in the Kansas City area, and they were shocked and saddened by it. The most gratifying thing was that I saw how clearly kids understood that this situation was about censorship and about violating the First Amendment. They understood that it was a threat to their freedom to read and my freedom to publish. One boy got his friends together and took about three thousand books out of his school district's libraries to show that if you remove what's controversial, you don't have very much left.

What was the hardest part for you?

The hardest part was going to the trial and listening to the school board talk about why they didn't think the book should be in the library. They said it was "shallow" and that it "glorified" and "promoted" homosexuality, and that it sent the wrong message to young people who read it. That was sad to hear. They said we're all sick and that homosexuality is evil and immoral, and that kids shouldn't be exposed to it. These are things I've heard my whole life, but it was worse hearing them said in a court of law. It felt as though what I am and what gay people are was being put on trial.

Did you feel as if you changed any minds?
I think both Sandy and I carved out some niches. For example, a woman who was frequently on Christian radio stations interviewed me during Sandy's and my first visit to Kansas City. I was also on a panel with her—on the opposite side, of course. Privately, she said to me that she thought it was a well-written book; she just didn't agree with it. And I think it was understood that had we met under different circumstances, we might have been friends. She saw Sandy and me together, and I think it taught her that we were not monsters. And perhaps she'll rethink her position gradually. I think we enabled a lot of people to get to know us a little— we went to Kansas three times—and I think maybe some of them have begun to understand that in many ways we're like they are. I don't think we convinced anybody who wanted the book burned in the first place, but I definitely feel that we made a difference to people who were less adamant.

What do you think really bothers them about the book?

That it ends happily. That it shows that gay people can fall in love and lead happy, productive lives and that we can contribute to society. That's what they call "glorification," when all it is is the truth. I think many homophobic people are terrified that if their children see that gays and lesbians can be happy, their children will want to be gay. They're sure homosexuality is a choice, and they seem to feel that teaching kids it's wrong will prevent them from being gay.

Your book has helped so many gay people. Do you have any advice for young people who might be struggling with some of the same things you did?

Understand that you're not the only one. And try to understand that the world is getting better. We're in the middle of a backlash now because gay issues are finally being addressed, but it *is* getting better. That's hard to believe when you're in pain, but it's really true that as you get older, it gets better. You have to hang on to the fact that you have every right to be here and to be exactly who you are. It's scary sometimes, but it can also be wonderful when you get out from under your parents or whoever is telling you that you're bad. You're not bad. You're a unique, special person, and you have a right to live your own life.

PINK PAGES: READING ABOUT THE GAY AND LESBIAN EXPERIENCE

Nancy Garden's *Annie on My Mind* (Farrar, Straus & Giroux, 1982) and her novel *Lark in the Morning* (Farrar, Straus & Giroux, 1991) are two of the many great novels for young adults featuring lesbian and gay characters. Some other fiction you might want to read includes:

Am I Blue?: Coming Out from the Silence (HarperCollins, 1994), edited by Marion Dane Bauer. This is a collection of short stories with gay themes written by some of the most popular writers of books for young adults, including M. E. Kerr, Gregory Maguire, Bruce Coville, Francesca Lia Block, and Lois Lowry.

The Arizona Kid (Little, Brown, 1988) by Ron Koertge. Over the course of a summer spent living with his gay uncle, a sixteen-year-old boy comes to understand more about what it means to be a gay person.

The Cat Came Back (Naiad Press, 1993) by Hillary Mullins. A seventeen-year-old tells her own coming-out story involving a teacher, her coach, and another student.

Crush (Alyson, 1988) by Jane Futcher. The story of a high school romance between two girls, this novel reflects both the joy and the pain of falling in love.

The Front Runner (William Morrow, 1974) by Patricia Nell Warren. Now considered a classic, this novel about a college track athlete coming out was one of the first books dealing honestly with the subject of a young person discovering his sexuality.

Jack (Macmillan, 1989) by A. M. Homes. When his father comes out as gay, Jack has to deal with his conflicting feelings and with telling his best friend. A very funny book.

Living in Secret (Bantam, 1993) by Cristina Salat. When Amelia's divorced parents get into a custody battle over her, she finds herself on the run as she has to change her identity in order to stay with her mother and her mother's lover.

The Man Without a Face (Lippincott, 1972) by Isabelle Holland. The moving story of a young man who learns a lot about accepting people—including himself—for who they are during a summer in which he forms a friendship with a reclusive man. This book was made into a movie starring Mel Gibson, but the plot of the movie deletes all references to homosexuality.

Night Kites (Harper Trophy, 1989) and *Deliver Us from Evie* (Harper Trophy, 1995) by M. E. Kerr. *Night Kites* is about a young man's struggle to accept his brother's homosexuality when he learns that his brother has AIDS. *Deliver Us from Evie* is the story of a lesbian teenager in a small farming town who challenges stereotypes, especially when she falls for the daughter of a prominent town leader.

Unlived Affections (Alyson, 1995) by George Shannon. While going through a box, a young man discovers a package of letters his father sent to his mother. By reading them, he learns the true reason for his father's leaving the family—his discovery of his own sexuality and his love affair with another man.

Weetzie Bat (HarperCollins, 1989) by Francesca Lia Block. The first in the series of Weetzie Bat books, this modern fairy tale looks at love in all its forms. Several of the books in the series feature gay characters, and the fifth book, *Baby Be-Bop* (1995), tells the life story of Weetzie's gay friend Dirk McDonald.

LESBIAN AND GAY FAST FACT **FOUR**

How Do I Know If I'm Gay or Lesbian?

Knowing whether or not you are gay is different for everybody. Some people know when they're very little. Others don't realize it until they're much older. It is not uncommon for people in their thirties and forties, and sometimes even in their sixties and seventies, to discover that they are lesbian or gay. This may sound strange, but the age at which a person accepts himself or herself is different for everyone.

Most of us who are gay realize it when we begin to develop attractions toward people of the same sex. Maybe you're a girl, and your friends are talking about some guy on the basketball team. But all you can think about is a certain girl in your Spanish class. Or perhaps while all of the guys are worrying about which girl to ask to the prom, you're thinking about the guy you'd like to ask to go.

Now, having crushes on people of the same sex doesn't automatically mean that you are gay. In fact, it isn't unusual for people suddenly to feel some kind of attraction toward a person of the same sex or to have sexual dreams about or even to experiment sexually with people of the same sex. Sometimes this is a normal part of growing up. But when these crushes continue, or when you just know that how you feel is more than a passing thought, that's when you should start to pay attention to what is going on.

Some gay people are tempted to have sex with the opposite sex just to see if they can. For example, a man who has sex with a woman may think this "proves" he isn't gay, even if he is mainly attracted to other men. But remember, being gay is not only about sex. It's what you feel inside that matters.

Remember, too, that you don't have to know everything about yourself right away. There is a lot of pressure in our society for people to label themselves as soon as possible. We like to know who and what people are, because not knowing makes us nervous. We also like to know what we are ourselves, so that we can say we belong to one group or another. Unfortunately, this makes it very hard for people to take the time they need to discover what is right for their lives. You don't have to categorize yourself if you don't want to, or if you aren't sure.

Realizing that you are gay is usually a process that occurs over a period of time. Sometimes something will happen and a person will suddenly realize that she or he is gay. But for most of us, it happens a little more slowly. Many gay people say that they felt "different" as young people—they didn't seem to be exactly like the other people around them. Then, as they learned more and more about themselves, they came to understand why they felt different. This doesn't mean that just because you feel different you must be gay. A lot of us feel different from the people around us. But it is a common feeling for a lot of gay and lesbian people.

If you really believe that you are gay, chances are you're right. Most people do not come to that conclusion without having thought about it a lot. But only you can know for sure. This isn't always easy. Sometimes what other people say or what we've been taught to believe gets in the way. But if you really listen to yourself, you will probably be able to tell.

DAN BUTLER
ACTOR

Actor Dan Butler is an anomaly in Hollywood—an openly gay actor in a business where fear of coming out of the closet keeps many lesbians and gay men silenced. Butler is a regular on the hit sitcom Frasier, *where he plays sportscaster Bob "Bulldog" Briscoe, and he has also appeared in numerous films. His one-man show,* The Only Thing Worse You Could Have Told Me, *based on his experiences as a gay man coming to terms with his sexuality, has wowed critics and audiences around the country.*

What was growing up like for you? Did you, like a lot of gay people, feel different?
I think I realized more in retrospect that I was gay. It was just a natural progression for me. I knew that I was attracted to men, but it felt so natural that I just took it for granted that everyone felt the same way. As I understand it, most men do go through a phase like that, where they are attracted to their buddies. It's always mystified me where the fork in the road occurs, where all of a sudden some guys start going out with girls—which I did for a while—

and where other guys maintain that attraction to other men. I never felt I was suppressing anything; I was just going through a natural evolution. I just realized that I was much more attracted to a couple of my male friends than I was to my girlfriend. Having a girlfriend was more of a status thing, because everyone did it.

So you never felt isolated or bad about being gay?
I never had a tortured feeling of hiding who I really was. Also, I didn't have the experience that some gay men have of being effeminate or of being somehow outwardly different from other people. I didn't have to deal with that. I'm amazed that people get through adolescence when they have to put up with that.

In an odd way, I think not sticking out can make things more confusing for some people. Sometimes having to go through being called names and having people pick on you when you're younger makes you question things about yourself that you wouldn't otherwise. Did you go through anything like that?
I think my biggest growth having to do with being gay came later in life. I got to the age of thirty and felt that even though I was an individual and had my own thoughts, certain areas of discussion or thought, ideas and philosophies, were just this

massive regurgitation of everyone else's thoughts. I didn't have a pure thought of my own. Being gay, and having to question my sexuality and who I was as a man, felt more pure, because I'd had to distill everything I'd ever heard about gay people and realize that it didn't jibe with my own experiences of myself.

This came about not only because of pressure from society as a whole but also from being part of a community of other gay men and women, some of whom were giving me the message that I had to be a certain way because I was gay. There are things I associate with and things I don't. I am very protective of my individuality, so anytime I feel I am being identified with a group, I balk. I don't want to be defined that way. I think ideally that what's important is being accepted as a person, and being gay is just a part of who that person is.

As an actor, did you worry about coming out?
The biggest public coming-out was doing my one-man show. After that, I felt like I was on for the ride, wherever it took me. Through it all, I try to keep my sense of humor and maintain the attitude that it really isn't such a big deal. Yes, one's sexuality and whom one loves is a very important thing, but it's not the overriding, defining point of who I am. It's just a part of who I am. Unfortunately, I think so much emphasis is put on it that you have to go

through an almost-schizophrenic stage where you put too much emphasis on sex, because it's been denied to you, and you have to go through your own declaration of independence of who you are.

Were you worried that doing the show might hurt your career?
I didn't think about it a lot. It was more frightening to me to go out there and be doing my own material, things I'd written, ideas I put forth, different characters I was portraying. I worried about whether or not it would mean anything to anyone. That was the terrifying part. The sexuality issue was just a part of all that. I put it, for lack of a better word, in God's hands. Some people might be uncomfortable with that idea, but in many ways it was a spiritual journey for me. I knew I had to just go for it.

Do you think the fear of coming out keeps a lot of performers in the closet?
I equate it with a lot of other fears in life that become such phantoms for people. If you always stay on the sidelines, thinking about what it's going to be like, you're never going to be able to walk through it and see the fear evaporate.

Does it feel good knowing that what you did might help someone else come out?

I think seeing other people's experiences does help. I hope that mine can help other people in some way. But when it comes down to it, you have to have your own experiences. Hopefully, you will have support from the friends you've chosen to surround yourself with, the people who really want you to be yourself completely, but you have to do it for yourself. I think my biggest argument against outing someone is that people think they know what's best for you. No one knows what's best for you except you, and taking a step like coming out has to come down to your being ready to do it, not from pressure from outside.

Did coming out damage your career at all?
I don't think so. I don't know what goes on behind the scenes, so I can't say for certain that I've never been the target of homophobia. But if I have, it hasn't affected me. I feel very fulfilled as an artist and as a man, and I'm excited about the creativity my work has brought about. I'm working in television. I'm working in movies. I'm working in the theater. I've got a terrific life in Hollywood.

How do you think your coming out has affected people you work with?
I really don't know. The only reference point I can have is how I feel and how I live my life. I try to be the best person I can be, and to challenge myself

as a creator and remind myself to have fun and enjoy life. It moves me that a lot of people have come up to me and told me I was influential in their decision to come out. That certainly feels wonderful, and it's an incredibly powerful effect to have. I'm always thankful when people write or tell me that I somehow helped them. What more can you ask for—not just as a gay person but as a human being—than to be of help to someone else? The worst thing you can do is to be ashamed of yourself, no matter who you are. So anything I can do to eradicate that is a wonderful thing.

Being ashamed is often about being afraid. Do you ever find yourself being afraid of things?
I hate when it happens in myself, because I have those knee-jerk reactions, too, sometimes. There is a reaction of fear to things that are different, instead of a reaction of curiosity. This doesn't mean you should walk into dangerous situations, but you should be open to things. That makes life richer.

I've redefined fear for myself. Usually when fear crops up, I know it's a sign that I should be doing that thing I'm afraid of. Then I try to turn it around and use it. I question why I'm fearful and try to see what will happen if I walk through the fear. I want to know how it will change my life or help me see things differently.

What have you learned most about yourself from these experiences, especially from doing the one-man show about your life?

It's a wonderful thing to listen to your life and to listen to what the voice inside of you wants you to do. I believe that when you get on track and follow what you want to do, then hidden hands come out and help you keep on track. When you take the initiative to do what you want to do, you will get help from unexpected sources. To do this, it's essential that you love yourself first. I think many gay people carry around a lot of anger, and it prevents them from really doing what they want to do. We need to let go of that.

But when you grow up being told that what you are is wrong or bad, isn't it natural to have a lot of anger about that?

It's very hard not to. I think a lot of it is whom you choose to surround yourself with, whom you choose to be your friends. Unfortunately, for everything bad that's been said about gay people, you can find an example of it in reality. For anything negative that's been said about any group of people, you can find someone who is an example of that bias. I love the richness and the creativity and the passion and the color of friends of mine who are gay. But things I don't like, and don't choose to be around, are acid gossiping and picking people apart, and the attitude that you should take what's been done to you to hurt you and use it against other people. I think it's really easy to be bitter and angry, and to pick at scabs and constantly complain about how everyone has hurt you. But it doesn't accomplish anything. There are too many people of amazing resilience and courage who have gone through the same things and emerged as strong individuals. If you hold resentment close to you, it's just going to hold you back. Anger is very powerful—there is power in any emotion, whatever it might be. But if you get stuck in that emotion, if it's the overriding emotion of your life, then you're going to be off balance.

Is your life now what you thought it would be like when you were a teenager?
When I graduated from high school, I was very apathetic. I think part of that was the time. Nixon was President. The Vietnam War was sort of smoldering to an end. I was growing up in Indiana. Even though I was involved in the arts and sports and school, I was just a little depressed about everything. I thought I knew everything there was to know, and that nothing could interest me.

I think it's important to do something at that age to jump start your life. Go out and travel. Do something to open up your eyes and find out what you want to do with your life. It's easy just to get depressed or hurt. I know it was really easy for my heart to be hurt then. It can be a confusing time, because you're not quite through with being a kid, but you're not quite an adult yet. I kept being reminded, and sometimes I didn't listen, that theater and acting and creativity were things I was interested in from a very young age. When I look at my life, I find that every important relationship, every important lover, every great lesson of growth, everything has come from the theater. It's important to listen to what your inner voice is telling you to do.

Did you ever think you couldn't be a successful actor because you were gay?
Everyone always wants to set up rules about can and can't, as though things can be defined that way. But those rules are always changing. Look at what's happened in our lifetime—rules about everything have been blasted apart. Saying people can't do something because they're gay is just a fashionable prejudice right now. Unfortunately, many people like to hate someone for something, and they're disappointed because all of their hates are being taken away one by one. This just happens to be one that's left. But that will change. Not that you should just sit back and wait for it to change. You should be vigilant and call people on certain things. But know that it will change. I think it's

exciting when issues—for instance, gay marriage—
come up and people get talking about them. It
forces you to stand up for yourself and to think
about what you really believe about an issue.

**Do you consciously try to affect the content of pro-
grams you do?**
Recently, I was reading the script for a film I was
thinking of doing. There was one scene where
someone called someone else an antigay name,
and I pointed out that it just wasn't something that
had to be there. It wasn't necessary to the story. So
they cut it. With *Frasier* the content is never a problem. So yes, if something negative was in a script, I
would say something about it, or just not be
involved with the project.

**Is Hollywood as homophobic as a lot of people say
it is?**
Of course there's homophobia in Hollywood, just
as there is everywhere. But I think sometimes people see it when it isn't really there. Sometimes not
getting a job isn't about being gay. The most quali-
fied person gets the job, or the person who looks
right. It's not always that there's some phantom out
there not casting you because of your sexuality.

**What do you think about the idea that only gay
actors should play gay roles?**

When people say that, I always think, Well, then more actors need to come out. There isn't exactly a big group of openly gay actors volunteering for gay roles. Anyway, I don't have a problem with people playing different roles. You should be able to play people who are unlike you. That's why it's called acting.

What do you like best about being part of the gay community?
I think what I like most about being gay is just that it's who I am. To completely embrace who I am and to be supportive of other people in my community who do the same thing is a great feeling. This doesn't mean that we all have to think the same way or like the same things or anything like that. We don't all have to go marching on Gay Pride Day or vote Democrat. It doesn't mean that at all. What it should mean is that we are free to be anything we want to be, and that we just happen to love people of the same sex because that's how we were created.

Don't you think that when some people first become part of a gay community, they want everyone to be a certain way—a "gay way"—because it makes them feel like part of a family?
I think we do question what it means to be gay. Is it a dress code? Is it how you look or act? I suppose

you have to go through that at first. You try on different things. And hopefully you find out what works for you and discard the rest. That's going to happen the rest of your life—you discard one set of things and move on to another. Ultimately what's important is that you do what makes you feel fulfilled and happy. You're always changing the things that mean something to you. Things you cared about last year might not interest you this year. You should always be opening yourself up and asking yourself what you learned today. I think it's important to surround yourself with creative people who inspire you, and whom you admire. The people you surround yourself with can be very important, because unfortunately many people don't have supportive families of their own. Fortunately, we have the ability to create families around us.

LIGHTS, CAMERA, ACTION: GAY AND LESBIAN LIFE ON FILM

While several television shows, including *Ellen* and *Frasier,* feature lesbian and gay characters, not every episode has a gay theme, and you can't always catch them when you want to see them. When you're in the mood to see something about gays and lesbians, you might consider renting one of the following films. They are all available on video, and they each have something to say about a different aspect of lesbian and gay life.

The Adventures of Priscilla, Queen of the Desert (1994). An Australian comedy about learning to love who you are. A group of drag-queen performers cross the desert in a giant pink bus on their way to a performance. Along the way, they find out more about themselves and one another than they ever thought possible.

Beautiful Thing (1996). A British movie about what happens when two boys come out to each other. Very realistic in depicting the changing and sometimes painful emotions that can arise from the pressures of being young and gay, this film is ultimately very positive.

The Birdcage (1996). Robin Williams and Nathan Lane star as an outrageous gay couple who agree to play it straight when Williams's son announces that he's engaged to the daughter of a homophobic politician. When the meeting between the two families starts to go horribly wrong, Williams, Lane, and their gay friends save the day.

Go Fish (1994). A gritty, almost-documentarylike movie about the ups and downs of a group of lesbian friends who spend a lot of time talking about love and what it means.

The Incredibly True Adventures of 2 Girls in Love (1995). What happens when a white girl from the wrong side of the tracks falls in love with an African-American girl from the right side of the tracks? The results are funny, touching, and very real in this story of first love between two teenage lesbians.

Philadelphia (1993). Tom Hanks won an Oscar for Best Actor for his work in this gripping drama about a man living with AIDS who sues the law firm where he once worked after they fire him. Loosely based on a true story.

To Wong Foo, Thanks for Everything, Julie Newmar (1995). If you've ever wondered what Wesley Snipes, Patrick Swayze, and John Leguizamo would look like as women, then this movie is for you. The three action heroes star as hilarious drag queens in this story of a town changed forever when these three "ladies" stop in for a visit.

LESBIAN AND GAY FAST FACT **FIVE**

What Is Homophobia?

Sometimes when we discuss issues about the gay community, we use the word *homophobia*. Homophobia is a hatred of gay and lesbian people just because they are gay, and homophobes are people who hate them.

But homophobia isn't really hatred. The word *phobia* means "a fear of" and is used to describe something we are afraid of. So homophobia is actually a fear of homosexuals.

The interesting thing about phobias is that they are also described as being irrational fears. In other words, they are fears that we have about what *might* happen. So homophobes are afraid of what lesbian and gay people might do. Sounds silly, right? Unfortunately, homophobia isn't funny. It can be very harmful. While homophobia can be as simple as someone telling a cruel joke about gay people, or calling someone a "faggot," it can also be much worse. Some gay and lesbian people have been killed just for being gay.

Homophobia can also be less visible. It can result in laws being passed that say gay people can't adopt children, as has been done in some parts of the United States. It can cause gay people to be portrayed in negative ways in movies or television shows. It can result in people saying that gay people shouldn't be around children.

What causes homophobia? Ignorance. Homophobes don't really know anything about gay people. They think they do, but the things they think they know are wrong. They might think that gay people try to "make" other people gay, or want to have sex with everyone around them. They might think that gay people aren't responsible citizens. They might think that gay people caused AIDS. None of these things is true, but homophobes will say they are. They may even claim to have proof of it.

Most of us are afraid of things that are different, especially people. We feel as if we can't understand someone because she comes from a different country, or even a different city. We think that we won't have anything in common with someone who doesn't look like we do. We let all kinds of things get in the way of getting to know one another. While it's okay to be afraid, it's not okay to let fear stop us from getting to know other people. If you take a chance and find out what a person is like, sometimes you discover a lot you never expected to.

Homophobes don't want to find out what gay people are like. It's easier for them to put lesbians and gays in a little box and believe that we are all the way they think we are. They're afraid that if they get to know us, they will find out that in some ways we are just like they are. And then they won't be able to hate us anymore. Most homophobes think they don't know anyone who is lesbian or gay. They think of gay people as faceless, with no personalities or feelings. This is what allows them to hate. It's also what makes them afraid.

How do we fight homophobia? There are several ways, but the best one is education. If people understand that gays and lesbians are just people, they can stop fearing them. And once they do this, they will stop hating them.

We can start educating people by not letting anyone around us tell jokes or make negative comments about gay people—or anyone, for that matter. If someone does say something, we can ask them why they said it. This isn't always easy, and it may not work at first, but eventually it may make people think about why they are telling jokes or making comments they shouldn't. And it may make them feel a little foolish. Then maybe they will think twice before saying something like that again. If you can get people thinking, that's a good place to start.

* * *

There are many groups within the lesbian and gay community that work to fight homophobia in our society. One of the most active is the Gay and Lesbian Alliance Against Defamation (GLAAD). GLAAD is a watchdog group that monitors television, film, radio, and print media for their portrayals of lesbian and gay people. It speaks out against negative portrayals of gays and lesbians, and it supports and encourages the realistic portrayal of gay people in the media. GLAAD also holds an annual awards ceremony honoring programs and actors portraying gays and lesbians in positive ways.

GLAAD has many offices around the country, and those addresses are listed below, by city. It also has a site on the World Wide Web that contains a wide variety of information about how gays and lesbians are being portrayed in the media, and provides information on how to write to sponsors who advertise on gay-positive shows, which shows feature gay-positive characters, and what efforts are being made by antigay groups to stop accurate portrayals of lesbians and gays. The address of the site is www.glaad.org.

P.O. Box 78707
Atlanta, GA 30357
Phone: (404) 876-1398

P.O. Box 146343
Chicago, IL 60614
Phone: (312) 409-2824

P.O. Box 7214
Kansas City, MO 64113
Phone: (816) 756-5991

8455 Beverly Boulevard, Room 305
Los Angeles, CA 90048
Phone: (213) 658-6775
Information hot line: (800) GAY-MEDIA

150 West 26th Street, Room 503
New York, NY 10001
Phone: (212) 807-1700

1010 University Avenue, Room 171
San Diego, CA 92103
Phone: (619) 688-0094

1360 Mission Street, Room 200
San Francisco, CA 94103
Phone: (415) 861-2244

1875 Connecticut Avenue NW, Room 800
Washington, DC 20009
Phone: (202) 986-1360

SARAH PETTIT
MAGAZINE EDITOR

In the early days of the gay rights movement, it wasn't possible to publish gay newspapers or magazines openly because of the fear surrounding being gay. So news and articles about being gay were often copied secretly and distributed by dedicated individuals who felt it was important for the information to be available.

At a time when having gay-oriented material mailed to your home might lead to being arrested, no one could imagine that one day there would be newspapers and magazines devoted to lesbian and gay people sold openly on newsstands, or that advertisers would take out ads in magazines for gay people, and that celebrities would want to be on the covers.

But today, most large cities do have their own gay newspapers, and there are a number of magazines that cover the life of the lesbian and gay community. The most successful of these is Out *magazine. When* Out *first debuted, in 1992, some people did not think a magazine totally dedicated to gay culture would make it. But* Out *proved them wrong. With a mixture of hard news about issues facing the gay community and articles about gay influences on the worlds of music, art, dance, theater, and writing, the magazine reflects the whole range of experiences lesbian and gay people have.*

Sarah Pettit is the editor in chief of Out magazine. After being involved with the short-lived but influential New York gay magazine OutWeek as a writer and editor, she was instrumental in launching Out, the first magazine for the gay community to be published by a mainstream company. As the editor in chief, she is responsible for overseeing the content and direction of the magazine, and this gives her a unique perspective on the changing nature of the gay community.

Were you aware of gay people when you were growing up?

I was in an interesting situation, because I had a relative who was close to my family who was gay, and who was pretty much accepted by my parents. She was my mom's youngest sister. She was kind of a mentor to me.

Did you know that you were gay yourself?

What's amazing about people, I think, is the remarkable degree of self-preservation many of us have, especially as gay people. There's this intelligence you have about things on an instinctual level, even if you don't totally understand them or understand what's going on with yourself. As a teenager, I didn't really know about the social concept of gayness. I'd heard people call other people "faggot" in school, and that kind of thing, but I'd been raised without a lot of prejudice about it in my family. What I'd had was this example of my aunt, who had been welcome in my family, and who was very supportive of me. That created a basis for me to be able to be free just to let the feelings of being gay come out in a less painful way than sometimes happens. None of this is to say that my teen years, from about fifteen to eighteen, were a picnic. I was at a boarding school where the overall atmosphere was extremely heterosexual.

How did you deal with your feelings?
I found my way of coping was really to follow my instincts. I gravitated toward the couple of teachers there who I sensed were gay, and kind of sought them out as a support group in a way. Since then, the school has developed a straight/gay alliance, but at the time that I was there, nobody was out. The teachers I went to weren't particularly out, but in small ways there was this mutual recognition where they understood that I was going to them for mentoring and that I understood that they were gay, even though they never said it. Because this was a boarding school, the teachers were in loco parentis; they were our legal guardians, so they really couldn't risk being out.

That period of my life—my adolescence—was

kind of a drag. I sought out places to feel supported. But this was a school where a lot of the kids were brainiacs, so it wasn't unusual to bury yourself in books and studying. But also because of that, there wasn't the social pressure to date and to go to proms and things like that. And during that period of time, I was sort of dating guys. I never felt entirely uncomfortable dating guys. It wasn't one of those things where I thought, Oh my God, I'm a lesbian and I don't want to be with this guy. I just felt that dating guys was an option, but it wasn't really where I was at.

How did you come to the realization that you were gay?
The way I got to the place of saying, "I'm gay," and coming out was very organic. I think it just naturally happened over the course of a two- or three-year period during my last years of high school. Then, my senior year of high school, I developed a crush on one of my female teachers. That's when my feelings of being an outsider translated more into feelings of being cognizant of the fact that I was gay, and different because of that.

Did it make you feel different from the people around you?
I read a lot of poetry. I walked in the woods a lot. I did things that, now that I look back on them,

made me stand out as a kind of loner. Not that I didn't fit in and have a lot of friends, but I always had this sense of being somehow apart.

Did you feel you couldn't talk to your friends about it?
No, I didn't really feel like that. I did tell my best friend in my dorm.

What did she say?
She was great. She was black in a very white school. She was someone who had dated marines by the time she was sixteen, and she had a tattoo, so all of the preppy kids where we were saw her as this other kind of strange being anyway. So I think she kind of understood something about not feeling part of the crowd. And we're still friends.

Did you talk to your aunt about any of this?
I spent a lot of time with her. But I don't think I ever talked to her about it, which is interesting. My main recollection of coming out was that no one would actually say the word *gay* to me. I never had one of those "So, you're gay—now how are you going to cope with it?" conversations with anyone.

Do you think that made it more difficult for you?
I don't think it was a bad experience. I think what it meant ultimately was a lot of people not asking

me to have answers, at a time when I clearly didn't have answers. I think that was very healthy. There may have been a bit of weird closetedness being projected onto me because no one spoke openly about gay issues, but I also think it was that people saw this sixteen-year-old kid and didn't want to lay any more on me. It was a good and a bad thing.

Did anything negative happen that made you feel unhappy about being gay?
My senior year, it was much clearer to me. And that year, I had a bad experience. I was seeing the school shrink because my parents were in the midst of getting divorced, and I was feeling gay and different, and all of that. And she caught wind of the fact that I was hanging out with some of my teachers, which was perfectly within the boundaries of school life. We all lived on the same campus, and it wasn't unusual for the teachers to take kids out to eat, or to the beach, or whatever. One of my teacher friends took me to a café, and I told the therapist about this. She then proceeded to go to the teacher and threaten her in some manner.

All of a sudden, this teacher, this friend, was acting kind of strange around me. And again, I knew instinctively that there were ways in which people could be intimidated about being gay. I knew that these teachers were intimidated. So I figured out that this therapist had said something, and I was very angry. I confronted her about it, and then I stopped seeing her as a therapist. It was pretty bad. But the good part of it was that I did have a basic sense of self-preservation. Because when I confronted the therapist, she essentially told me that because I was a minor, I didn't have any rights anyway, and I said, "It may be the law, but I don't have to put up with this." So in that sense, it taught me that I could stand up for myself if someone tried to use being gay against me.

Do you remember thinking that you wanted to be part of the gay community at some point later in your life?
My progression as a gay person was in many ways very direct. I graduated from high school. I went home for the summer and dated a couple of guys. And I sort of enjoyed that. But when I got to college, it was very funny. I think I was there maybe four or five days, and I walked up to the guy on campus who looked the most gay to me, and I said, "Excuse me, you're gay, aren't you?" And he said, "Yes." And I said, "Well, then take me to where the gay people are." He took me to a party, and I met the first woman I dated there. It was all very direct. I think I felt like I'd been waiting long enough and it was time.

Was your experience at college a good one?

I was very, very fortunate in that I went to a university that had a very progressive, cool student body. It was a very interesting time then, and it was a very, very exciting time for me. I worked for the gay student group there and ran the gay and lesbian awareness days and things like that. I worked to have the school's nondiscrimination clause changed to include sexual orientation. Things like that.

Did you always plan on using your skills for the gay community?
People always say to me, "Do you feel your life is too narrow because you work on this gay magazine and within the gay community?" Since I was eighteen or nineteen, the things that have interested me intellectually and the things that have interested me personally have blended. The issues that I feel very passionate about have melded with more generic things, like having a job and making a living. What I was interested in in college was literature and books and languages and political activism. And I've been lucky to find a career that combines my interest in writing, stories, and people with this interest in gay issues. That's what this magazine is for me. So in many ways, I have the best of both worlds. I get to do this thing that I feel very passionate about, but it has really practical applications, as well.

Do you think that being so out in school allowed you to see this as a possibility?

The thing about college—and I think this happens at different places at different times—was that there really was this incredible sense of being part of the cool crowd as a gay person. People wanted to come to our parties. People wanted to know what we were doing. This isn't to say it was always a rosy picture. There were gay bashings. I almost got into a fight with a member of the football team because he tore down a poster for one of our dances. Things like that did happen. But people were interested in us, and I think that made us feel positive about ourselves and feel that we were part of this interesting group of people.

Do you think that happens to a lot of people once they leave high school and go to college?

College is an interesting time, because you have all of these people coming together who have spent a long time feeling alone and apart from other people like themselves. Then they find themselves in a place where they can have friends and can express themselves openly. That's something you don't really have in high school. It can be a very liberating experience.

And I don't think that experience is limited to those of us who go to colleges with active gay groups. I think you find it when you join any group that allows you to be yourself. You can find that same sense of freedom in groups like ACT-UP or the Lesbian Avengers. That's the power of gay groups. It's in gay choruses and lesbian softball leagues. It happens when people who have been made to feel that they're the only ones are able to come together and be part of a community.

Do you get tired of always working on gay issues?
I go through periods. Thankfully, there is a lot of material to make a gay magazine out of. There are a lot of people doing really interesting things. Some of the most dramatic issues of our time— whether they're health issues or legal issues or civil rights issues—happen within the context of this community. That's a lot of drama for a magazine to cover. I don't get tired of it because there's a lot of stimulation. I do, however, think it's important to keep yourself extended into the world. I'm pretty vigilantly pro-gay, but I do think we should know what's going on in the larger world around us.

Do you find yourself acting as a spokesperson of sorts because of your job?
It's pretty hard for me not to, because as soon as someone asks me what I do, the gay issue comes up. Recently, I was having my teeth cleaned, and the woman doing it asked me how I could stand being around straight men, because they're so

awful. I told her one of my best friends is a straight man, and she was very surprised, because she assumed that because I'm gay, I couldn't be friends with this straight person or be interested in him and his world. And I think that's something that the next generation of gay people has a better handle on—the idea that being really healthy about yourself and being out doesn't mean that you have to be totally apart from the world. I'm not against separatism. I think separatism is groovy and important in its own way, but there are different historical times when it's appropriate. And I think this is a time when it's less necessary for young gay people to cut themselves off. I think now is a time when straight and gay kids can hang out and be cool about one another and not have it be such a big deal.

What do you like best about being part of the gay community?
Maybe this is an antiquated idea, but I think that as a group of people, we're really special. It's like if I could pick any after-school group I wanted to belong to, I'd still pick the gay group. It's a pretty amazing group of people. When you look at the level of different experiences we've had, and how that crazy filter we all share of coming out and having to find our own ways in this world has made us different people, it's really exciting. I feel very

proud of being gay. I still feel like I'm part of the coolest club. If you spend a lot of time getting to where you feel comfortable with being gay, it makes you a really interesting person.

I think that's why I do what I do. I still feel that if I can be in a position to get a lot of great stories out to people, then I'm doing something really important. I feel that this magazine is a way to reach out to people every month and say, "Don't forget about this," or "Don't despair; have a sense of humor." It's a way of reminding people that they're a part of something that's really big and really important, and it feels wonderful to be involved with that.

THE NEWSSTAND: MAGAZINES FOR THE GAY COMMUNITY

There are many magazines for and about the gay community. Some of these, such as *Out* and *The Advocate*, are often available at public libraries. Many are found at newsstands, and all are available by writing to the publishers and asking for subscription information.

The Advocate. 6922 Hollywood Boulevard, 10th Floor, Los Angeles, CA 90028. A biweekly newsmagazine featuring the latest news of interest to gays and lesbians, as well as articles, interviews, and reviews of books, films, and music.

Amethyst: A Journal for Lesbians and Gay Men. 191 Howard Street NE, Atlanta, GA 30317. Features articles, fiction, poetry, photography, and essays relating to the gay experience.

Art & Understanding: The International Magazine of Literature and Art about AIDS. 25 Monroe Street, Albany, NY 12210. Features essays, articles, interviews, photography, and reviews of art and literature related to or inspired by the AIDS crisis.

Christopher Street. P.O. Box 1475, Church Street Station, New York, NY 10008. Features essays, articles, and fiction by gay men and of interest to them.

Curve. 2336 Market Street, Suite 15, San Francisco, CA 94114. A glossy lifestyle magazine featuring articles, essays, interviews, and news of interest to lesbians.

Genre. P.O. Box 18449, Anaheim, CA 92817-8449. For gay men, this slick magazine features articles, interviews, entertainment reviews, and short fiction.

Girlfriends. 3415 Cesar Chavez, Suite 101, San Francisco, CA 94110. A progressive magazine for lesbians, featuring articles, interviews, and essays about sex, politics, health, and entertainment.

Lambda Book Review. 1625 Connecticut Avenue NW, Washington, DC 20009. A review of lesbian and gay books and issues of interest to gay writers, readers, publishers, and booksellers.

Out. 110 Greene Street, Suite 600, New York, NY 10012. This magazine for both lesbians and gay men features articles, interviews, and essays about many different topics, ranging from politics to fashion, entertainment to sports.

Poz. P.O. Box 1279, Old Chelsea Station, New York, NY 10113-1279. A magazine written by and for people living with HIV/AIDS. Features articles, essays, and interviews about HIV/AIDS–related topics.

XY. 4104 24th Street, #900, San Francisco, CA 94114-3615. Exclusively geared toward gay men under the age of twenty-five, this glossy magazine features articles and columns about music, sex, culture, politics, and more.

LESBIAN AND GAY FAST FACT **SIX**

Don't All Lesbians Look Like Truck Drivers, and Don't All Gay Men Like Ballet?

We often have ideas about what people are like before we even meet them. These impressions may come from things we've heard or seen, or just from things we've made up in our heads. We believe that people will act in or look certain ways because they belong to groups that we think we know all about, when really we don't know anything about them.

These ideas are stereotypes—images we have of people based on things we think we know about them, or things we think are true. Stereotyping people is what we do when we make assumptions about them, like when we say that a guy must be stupid because he's a jock, or that a girl must be dumb because she's blond. We don't really know anything about these people except that one likes to play sports and one has blond hair, yet we assume things about them because of what we see on the outside. The problem with stereotypes is that they make us believe things about people before we let ourselves get to know them. And at times, people are discriminated against because of what others *think* they're like.

There are many stereotypes about gay and lesbian people: All lesbians look like men; all gay men are effeminate; all lesbians hate sex; all gay men are bad at sports. Many people assume these things are true, including many gay people. In fact, some people don't want to be gay because they believe it means they have to be these things, and other people think they can't be gay because they aren't any of these things.

Gay people come in all shapes and sizes, and they have every kind of personality imaginable. Some are quiet and some are loud. Some like sports and some don't. There is no one way to be gay or lesbian. Some lesbians have long hair and wear dresses; others have never worn anything but jeans. Some gay men like cooking; others like to climb mountains. Many like to do all of these things. We're all different, just like all straight people are different.

Sometimes there may be some truth to a stereotype, although it has usually been blown way out of proportion. This is true with gay stereotypes, too. No, not all gay men were part of the drama club in high school. But a lot were. Not all lesbians like to play softball. But many do. Often these kinds of activities attract gay and lesbian people because they provide an opportunity for us to be ourselves in a comfortable environment.

The important thing to remember if you are a gay person is that being gay doesn't limit who you are or what you can do. You can be on the baseball team or the cheerleading squad. You can wear what you like to and look the way you want. If the way you look or the things you like seem stereotypical, that's fine. If they don't, that's fine, too. Stereotypes are limiting only if you allow them to be.

DR. MARTIN PALMER
DOCTOR

*For people just discovering the gay community, it is some-
times difficult to understand where the community came
from and how life has changed for gay people over the
years. Dr. Martin Palmer has a unique perspective on the
gay community. During the past forty years, he has seen
it change dramatically from a secretive, primarily underground movement in the 1950s to one that, today, vocal-
ly challenges society's views of lesbian and gay people and
demands equality. He served in the army during World
War II, and for the last three decades he has been a doctor in Anchorage, Alaska, actively involved in one of the
greatest challenges ever to face the gay community—the
AIDS crisis. Now seventy-one, he continues to practice
medicine, and he also teaches English at the University of
Alaska at Anchorage.*

**When you were first becoming aware of being gay,
as a young man, did you ever dream that you would
be part of a gay community?**
There really was no such thing as a gay community,
at least not one anyone talked about, when I was

first discovering that I was gay. When I look back on that time—and I was very, very young when I started to realize I was gay—I remember feeling that I was different, and I understood *how* I was different, even though there really wasn't a word for it, as far as I knew. I did have access to my father's medical library, and I was able to look up some clinical information about homosexuality. Unfortunately, being gay was talked about as if it were a pathology. Back then, what little information that was available was almost all negative, and it was disturbing for me as a young man to read it. Everywhere I looked, it said I was sick. People then thought that the reason a person was gay was because she or he had grown up abnormally, with a smothering mother or a distant father or something. Well, I was very close to my father, and my mother died shortly after I was born, so that didn't fit. Besides, I was perfectly happy in my relationship with my father, who was a loving man.

As you got older, did you try to find other gay people?
You know, people talk about how there were never any role models for us to see, and there weren't on the surface. I looked in books for mentions of gay people, and there just weren't any. But as I got older, I realized that some of the people around me were gay. Then I discovered that there was an

extensive underground gay community, at least in the cities. I would go to New York when I was a young man, and I had a huge family of gay friends there. We had wonderful parties, and I knew all kinds of fascinating people. The gay community was very large and thriving there, but it just wasn't open or talked about.

You were also in the military for a time as a young man.

Almost all the men of my age were. I went in when I was eighteen, during World War II. We were training for the invasion of Japan.

Gay people in the military is such a hot issue now. What was it like being gay in the military then?

It wasn't even discussed. But you knew who was gay. Right after the surrender of Japan, I was sent to occupied Japan. And I soon found out who in my unit was gay. There were many men I met there whom I was friends with for years. But all of this happened under the watchful eyes of the military, so we kept it all very quiet. We weren't afraid of being caught, really, but we knew we should keep it quiet.

What about when you went to medical school?

I graduated from Johns Hopkins Medical School in 1954. When I was there, there were a number of gay people, and we all knew one another. But it was still all undercover then. Remember, back then all of the textbooks said that we were sick, that something was wrong with us. And that's how most of society viewed homosexuals. Now, the school I went to was supposed to be a liberal one, and the faculty was progressive, but being gay was still something that wasn't discussed openly.

What did you and the other gay students think about these books that said you were sick?
We thought they were ridiculous. I had several close gay friends, and we would go all over the place together and do all kinds of what were considered gay things. So it wasn't as if we were living in secret all the time. But back then, many gay people, especially men, would later get married and have families, because it was what was expected of you. It wasn't at all like today, where you can be out and nobody—or very few people—cares.

How did it affect you, being told that being gay was a psychological disorder?
All you could do was live your life in the best way you could. Looking back, I think everyone who was gay then took at one time or another what we called the "talking cure," which was going for psychoanalysis to discover what caused our homosexuality. I remember going and constantly arguing with the

doctor about being gay. He said I was resisting
changing and refusing to be mature and responsible, and all kinds of things. We fought hard, but
I won.

**But did you ever really think there was anything
wrong with you?**
No, I didn't. Of course, I had to conceal being gay,
but I didn't think there was anything wrong with it,
because I was happy with who I was, and I knew I
wasn't sick. I just thought that other people didn't
understand it.

Did you think you couldn't be a doctor and be gay?
I didn't think I could be a doctor and be out. I
assumed I would always have to be quiet about who
I was, at least to people who weren't also gay. But at
the same time, I had a very active gay life. I was living in New Orleans at the time, and there was a
large gay community.

When did you move to Alaska?
I came up here in 1968 to work in a clinic. I didn't
know anybody here, and it took me about six
months even to find a gay group. At that time, they
were pretty closeted. But now, almost thirty years
later, things are dramatically different. The gay
community here is extremely active and vocal.
Watching life for gay people evolve over the course

of the 1970s and 1980s was spectacular, particularly the 1970s, when gay people really started to become political.

Did you ever have fear that, as a doctor working in what was a fairly isolated part of the country, you couldn't let people know you were gay?
Yes, I did. But as time went by, I found myself coming out in my daily life. I didn't put an ad in the paper saying I was gay or anything, but all of my associates knew, and all of my straight friends knew, and it was just a gradual, natural thing.

Are you out to your patients?
I am certainly out to anybody who asks. I don't conceal that I'm gay, and I'm associated with gay causes here in Anchorage, so most people know me.

In terms of your medical practice, when did you find yourself becoming more directly involved with the gay community?
It was definitely because of the AIDS crisis. In terms of being part of the medical community, AIDS just burst upon the scene almost overnight, and anyone who was involved with medicine and who had any gay patients was involved with it.

How has that affected you personally?
I had many friends here, and many patients, who

had AIDS. And almost all of them are dead now. It has been tremendously painful for me, because not only do I watch people I love die but I'm also in the fight as a doctor, and it's very hard to see something destroy so many people and not be able to stop it.

How does it affect you, as someone who lived through the early fight for gay rights, to see all of the things you worked for end with a large part of your community gone because of AIDS?
It's a sorrow that nothing can alleviate. It's there on the edge of my mind every single day. I think about those people, and I miss them and I love them. My friends are nearly all gone, and I mourn them all the time. I'm not hindered or stopped by the grief, but not a day passes that I don't think about all of the wonderful people who aren't here today. Now, there's nothing you can do but look at what's left and help in any way you can to see that it doesn't happen again to those people who are just now coming out.

Do you think the period around the 1960s, when so much was happening in the opening up of the gay community, was a more interesting time to be part of the gay community, even though it was more secretive?
We were a very vibrant community, and there was

something special about being a part of it. And even though we weren't out, we were still very angry about anything antigay. I remember the year I graduated from medical school, we would all gather around the television to watch Senator McCarthy—who at that time was in the midst of his anti-Communist and antigay attacks on artists and other people—get shot down, so to speak, by the people who stood up against him. And we just clapped and clapped, because we hated him and what he stood for. We were very opposed to people like McCarthy or his pal Roy Cohn, the attorney who was so viciously antigay but was gay himself. We couldn't wait to see them knocked down. And they were.

Now there is an active, visible gay community. What was it like for you living when there wasn't one?

I remember, when I lived in New Orleans, walking with my friends and going by the newsstand to look at the covers of the male-model magazines, "the physique magazines," as they called them then. But we didn't dare buy them. There was a man in town who had a huge collection of them, and he used to let us make appointments to come over to his apartment to look at them. Now you can go to almost any store and buy gay magazines, but back then we would never have thought of it.

Do you think that there has been any loss of community by being more visible?
I'm all for the openness we have now. The suppression and oppression we had then led to so many bad things for so many people. Although we had our own world, which was very lively, it was also filled with people who were very unhappy because they had to hide. I wouldn't want to go back to that.

Do you think younger gay people romanticize the early days of gay liberation too much?
I think it's a mistake to think that it was the perfect time, or that any other time was the perfect time. You aren't there. You're here. And to think that it could be re-created now is also a mistake. Whether people realize it or not, they are creating their own decades now, and that's what's important to focus on.

What has been the best part for you of being involved with the gay community for such a long time?
The best part has been looking back on my life and seeing what it has been like and what I've done. Now, it's looking ahead to what I still can do and still want to do to help the community.

Do you think that you can be gay and not be

involved in the gay community?
I think it's very hard. Once you come out, you find yourself getting more and more involved with gay people and gay things. You just can't help it, if you have any interest at all in what it means to be gay. It's who you are, and it's where you belong. I do know gay people who aren't part of the community, but for the most part, these people are not very happy, because they don't have a circle of people to share their lives with openly and freely. This doesn't mean you have to be involved in every gay organization or be marching in parades, or anything like that. It means that as a gay person, you are probably going to want other gay people in your life. And when you start finding those people, you quickly find that you are a community.

Is your life now what you imagined it would be like when you were first coming out?
That's a question I can't answer. It is what it is. When I was thirteen or fourteen, I thought I would get married and have children, because that's what everyone did. So my life is definitely different in that respect, and I'm very glad for it. But everything that's happened, and where it's all taken me, is just a result of my experiences, and there was no way I could have imagined everything that's happened to me.

What do you think has been the biggest change in the gay community over the years?

Definitely coming out, being able publicly to have an organized gay life. It thrills me to see those huge Gay Pride celebrations every year. I still remember my first one, in San Francisco in the early seventies. I just stood there and watched this group of two hundred thousand people celebrating being gay, and it was a feeling I can never fully describe. It was something I never thought I'd see in my lifetime. You just wouldn't have dared do that when I was coming out.

You know, I hear people say they don't understand why gay people have to make such a big deal about being gay—why we have to have parades and gay organizations and whatnot—and I think that they just don't understand. Being quiet about who you are causes such misery. I knew people who killed themselves rather than live with the torture of being told something was wrong with them. And it wasn't that they were weak people—they just couldn't stand the pressure of being told every day of their lives that they didn't deserve to be happy, that they were abnormal or sick. I don't want anyone to have to live like that ever again.

Do you think there will ever be a time when gay people are seen as "just like everybody else"?

No, I don't. We *are* different. Our outlook is different. And I don't want to be like everybody else. I think we are a very special community, and I think we should be proud of our differences. I hope that I will live another twenty-five years so that I can see where the gay community will be then, because I think it will be even more wonderful than it is now, especially for young gay people.

How do you feel, as someone who can look back over more than six decades of history, about what's happened in the gay community?
I look back in amazement. I love to look back and remember what was happening at different times. Very often, something I see or hear or read will set off a cascade of memories, and I remember all over again what it was like to do different things or know different people over the years.

How do you think young gay people can help make a difference in what happens to the gay community?
I think young gay people need to do their best to develop a historical sense of where the gay community has been at different times and where it's going. History is very important. Without understanding where you come from as a community, you can't help to move that community forward.

UNCOVERING HISTORY

The history of the gay and lesbian community is a fascinating one. All too often, though, gay people have been written out of history. More and more, lesbian and gay people are researching the community's past and writing about it to make sure people know about the contributions made by gay people. The books listed below are great places to start exploring gay history and the roles lesbians and gays have played in world history, as well. Some of these books cover the history of the lesbian and gay community in general; others look at the lives of specific groups of people within the gay community.

About Time: Exploring the Gay Past (Meridian, 1991) by Martin Duberman.

Coming Out Under Fire: The History of Gay Men and Lesbians in World War Two (Plume, 1991) by Allan Bérubé.

Creating a Place for Ourselves: Lesbian, Gay, and Bisexual Community Histories (Routledge, 1997), edited by Breet Beemyn.

The Gay Almanac (Berkeley Publishing Group, 1996), compiled by the National Museum Archive of Gay and Lesbian History.

Gay American History: Lesbians and Gay Men in the USA (Meridian, 1992) by Jonathan Ned Katz.

The Gay and Lesbian Liberation Movement (Routledge, 1992) by Margaret Cruikshank.

Gay Militants: How Gay Liberation Began in America, 1969–1971 (St. Martin's Press, 1995) by Donn Teal.

Hidden from History: Reclaiming the Gay and Lesbian Past (Meridian, 1989), edited by Martin Duberman, Martha Vicinus, and George Chauncey, Jr.

Liberation Was for Others: Memoirs of a Gay Survivor of the Nazi Holocaust (Da Capo Press, 1997) by Pierre Seel.

Long Road to Freedom: The Advocate History of the Gay and Lesbian Movement (St. Martin's Press, 1995), edited by Mark Thompson.

Making History: The Struggle for Gay and Lesbian Equal Rights 1945–1990 (HarperCollins, 1992) by Eric Marcus.

Men with the Pink Triangle: The True Life-and-Death Story of Homosexuals in the Nazi Death Camps (Alyson, 1994) by Heinz Heger.

No Baths but Plenty of Bubbles: An Oral History of the Gay Liberation Front, 1970–1973 (Cassell, 1996) by Lisa Power.

Odd Girls and Twilight Lovers: A History of Lesbian Life in Twentieth-Century America (Penguin, 1991) by Lillian Faderman.

Out of the Past: Gay and Lesbian History from 1869 to the Present (Vintage, 1995) by Neil Miller.

The Pink Triangle: The Nazi War Against Homosexuals (Henry Holt, 1986) by Richard Plant.

Stonewall (Dutton, 1993) by Martin Duberman.

LESBIAN AND GAY FAST FACT **SEVEN**

Don't All Gay People Get AIDS?

One of the biggest myths about gay people—especially gay men—is that we all have AIDS, or that we caused AIDS. AIDS is a disease. It affects both straight and gay people. In fact, AIDS is now infecting straight people at a higher rate than it is gay people, and women at a faster rate than men. But these facts really do not matter. In the end, we are fighting a disease, and it doesn't matter who has it.

When the AIDS crisis began in the early 1980s, the first people to be diagnosed with the disease were gay men. (In fact, the original name for AIDS was GRID, or Gay-Related Immune Deficiency, because only gay men were found to have it. It was also called "gay cancer.") And for several years, people believed that only gay men would get it. Now we know that isn't true.

No matter where it came from or who gets it, the fact is that AIDS has changed the gay community forever. Some of those changes have been good ones. Others have been bad. AIDS has brought us together as a community to work on a common issue. But it has also killed many of us.

There are ways to fight AIDS, and to stop it from controlling your life. The first is to educate yourself about safer sex. This means learning how HIV, the virus that causes AIDS, is—and isn't—spread. It means learning how to use condoms correctly. It also means learning how to respect yourself, so that you don't risk being exposed to AIDS. There are several good books about AIDS that can answer common questions about this disease. You can also get information from your local gay community center or health center.

The other way to fight AIDS is to become involved with one of the many AIDS-related organizations across the country. Most cities have groups that help fight AIDS, and they are always looking for volunteers. You can do anything, from working in the office to being a buddy to someone with AIDS. Some AIDS groups provide meals for people with AIDS; others walk the pets of AIDS patients. You can also help out by participating in an AIDS walk or bike ride, or by sponsoring someone else who does it.

AIDS will always be frightening, but it doesn't have to be overwhelming. Learn what it is and what it isn't, because the more you learn about it, the more you will realize that this is something we all deal with, and something we can all fight. It isn't about being gay or straight, white or black, poor or rich. It's about being human.

Getting the facts about AIDS is as easy as picking up the phone or reading a book. If you have questions about AIDS and need answers right away, call the National AIDS Hot Line at (800) 342-AIDS. They are open twenty-four hours a day, and they can provide you with the latest information.

There are also numerous books about AIDS that can give you all of the information you need about what the disease is and how to avoid becoming infected with HIV. The books listed below are good places to start.

AIDS & HIV: Risky Business (Enslow, 1997) by Daniel Jussim.

AIDS: Trading Fears for Facts (Consumer Reports Books, 1992) by Dr. Karen Hein.

AIDS: What Does It Mean to You? (Walker & Co., 1995) by Margaret O. Hyde and Elizabeth H. Forsyth.

100 Questions & Answers about AIDS: What You Need to Know Now (Beech Tree, 1993) by Michael Thomas Ford.

The Voices of AIDS (Morrow, 1996) by Michael Thomas Ford.

JENIFER LEVIN
MOTHER AND WRITER

One of the things many gay people think they have to give up is having families of their own. Society teaches us that families are made up of a mother and a father and children. But more and more, families do not look like that. Nowhere is this more evident than in the gay community, where lesbians and gay men are having their own children. Sometimes these children are biological; often they are adopted.

Some people believe that gay people shouldn't have children because the youngsters' families will be different from those of many of their friends and peers and this will confuse them. But studies done on children raised by gay people show that often they grow up happier and more well adjusted than children in "traditional" homes.

Still, there is a great deal of opposition to gay people raising children. While gays cannot be prevented from having children of their own, it is still sometimes very hard legally for them to adopt children in this country, and often in divorce cases where one parent is gay or lesbian, that person is not awarded custody of the children.

An increasing number of gay people who want to have

children are looking overseas, to countries such as China, Japan, and Russia, where there are many children waiting to be adopted. Jenifer Levin is one of these people. She and her partner, Julie, have adopted two children from Cambodia. The family lives in New York, where Jenifer is a writer. She is the author of four novels—Water Dancer, Snow, Shimoni's Lover, *and* The Sea of Light—*as well as a collection of short stories*—Love and Death, and Other Disasters.

What were your teenage years like?
They were really miserable. I was definitely one of those suicidal gay teenagers we hear about. I used to write in my diary, "Oh please, God, don't make me homosexual." These days, it sounds so absurd, given that there *are* support groups like P-FLAG and gay youth groups. But I think that sort of despair—of recognizing that you're different, and that the difference will permeate your whole life and never go away—is very hard, even if there *is* support. In some ways I was a very sensitive kid, and in others ways I was really clueless. But by the time they're teenagers, most people are getting at least a hint of who they are sexually, and I know that was definitely true for me.

Did you tell anybody?
No, I didn't. I know that I very much *wanted* to be like everybody else, and it was clear that I wasn't

going to be. My high school years were actually better than the years in junior high, which were full of genuine despair. I looked really different from my peers and was treated differently. At one point, some kids from school threw rocks at me as I was walking home. Mine was a miserable existence; I truly wanted to die. Groups of older kids would constantly yell at me, "Are you a boy or a girl?" and things like that. It was really depressing, and I felt that I had nowhere to turn.

How did you deal with it?
Getting into my later teen years was better, because I went to a large high school, and people split off into different social groups. So there was less social taunting and tormenting, but there still was this ominous, overwhelming sense of alienation and otherness. It wasn't until I went off to college that I started to see the possibilities of having a decent life as a gay person. There were lesbian teachers as well as lesbian students—this was during the early to mid-seventies, at the University of Michigan, which was a much bigger place than high school. The whole hippie thing was still going on. It helped me to see that there was hope for my life.

But I don't think I acknowledged the fact that I was queer and likely to remain so—and that's what I was; it was my destiny—until I was in my early twenties. For me, this struggle for acceptance lasted about eight years, from the time I was thirteen or fourteen. I was falling in love with girls. Even in early childhood, I always thought I would grow up and marry a girl—I knew *that* was weird and different. I remember telling my best friend when I was five or six that I wanted to marry her, and she said, "You can't do that." I asked her why, and she said, "Because we're both girls." I didn't understand that at all. I was sure she was wrong, because it seemed perfectly natural to me. From then on, there was a steadily increasing awareness of essential difference until I was about twenty-two or so. It was a battle, although it seems sort of antiquated now to say that. I'm glad that at least in places like New York there is consciousness about these issues.

You call yourself "queer," which is a word many of us had used against us when we were growing up. Do you find it powerful to reclaim it and use it to define yourself?
I really like the word *queer* because it embraces a genuine sense of the difference, the otherness, most of us felt growing up. And being gay—being queer—is so much more than just being homosexual. It's a distinct sense of being outside something, looking in.

Do you think it's easier now for people who, like yourself, felt so different at a young age?

There's more discussion now. And so many more
people are openly trying to live out their options
and really, really trying to be free. The fight is
always inside oneself, and to that extent, we're free
or we're not free, depending on how much we've
accepted who we are. But there are still many people who are oppressed because they aren't free
inside. To be free in so *many* ways—not just free to
be queer—is my ongoing struggle in life. That's a
difficult path, because it involves constant soul-
searching and change. And this search is both
enhanced and complicated by the presence of children in my life, because that's a very different kind
of love and tenderness.

**Was having children something you wanted but
thought you couldn't do?**
I have a peculiar history in that way. I was a Zionist
in my youth, and I went to live in Israel for a couple of years, where I became imbued with a sense
of responsibility to procreate and continue the
Jewish race—because we have been so destroyed by
so many things. There's a kind of paranoia in
thinking that the world is against you, is out to get
you, and that at the very least you have to be
extremely well defended against any attack. In
some ways, it fit in really nicely with my alienated
feelings about being queer and having the world
against me because of *that*. But my Zionism was

also in direct opposition to my being queer, because my understanding was that if I wanted to be part of my people in Israel, then I had to be heterosexual, as well. Now I see many more options there, but that's how I felt then. So I also thought then that, because I wasn't heterosexual, having children wasn't a possibility.

What made you change your mind?
I really liked the idea! It wasn't well thought out in the beginning, but I don't believe the urge to have children ever really is. It's just one of those things that comes over you, not a rational desire. It's all emotion and stamina and love and filling a need— at least that's what it is for me. If you really *thought* about how much work goes into raising a child, you'd probably never do it.

How did you come to adopt?
I first thought about having a child in my late twenties, but the wish didn't become a reality until I met my partner, Julie, whom I have been with for nine years. I expressed to her, early on, that I wanted to have a child. I'd always thought that would be a biological child. But several years into our relationship, we wound up going to Cambodia and we spent some time there. Then I got the idea of adopting a Cambodian child, because we both had some knowledge of the country and of the culture,

and we have a really strong emotional attachment to the people there. The idea of adoption seemed much more practical to me than having my own. Emotionally, too, it felt right. I adopted my first child, Makara, in 1994, and Julie adopted a second child in early 1996.

Had you thought about adopting in the United States?
I'd thought about it. But if I was going to adopt as an openly gay woman living with another openly gay woman, which I wanted to do, the options were almost nonexistent. I could possibly adopt an HIV-positive child, or I could explore an extraordinarily expensive type of private adoption through a lawyer. But I didn't have the money or the stamina to do either of those things.

What if you had pretended to be a single mother?
I could have. But the laws are set up so that if you lie on an application, the child can be taken away from you. So I never wanted to do that. Besides, I *intended* to be open. I thought it was very important that I do this as an openly gay person.

Is foreign adoption easier for gay people?
In some ways. I started the process in 1992 and adopted in 1994. You have to go through home studies, and you have to get approval and clear-

ance from the Immigration and Naturalization Service and all of that. None of it's very difficult—it's just a matter of taking all of these bureaucratic steps one at a time. Then when all the paperwork was done, I had to go overseas and start the process there. Julie had to leave after a few weeks, and I stayed for another three months, going through the Cambodian legal adoption process. Finally, it was officially approved, and Mak and I returned home together. He was three years old.

Was there ever any problem with your being queer?
The notion of people of the same sex living together in a relationship has a very different sort of cultural currency in Cambodia than it does here. The home study doesn't say these people are homosexual; it just says that these two people are a couple and that they live together. It's as simple as that.

Were you able to adopt as a couple?
No, I had to adopt as a single parent because gay marriage is not recognized. And Julie has also adopted our other son, Vannarith, as a single parent. Recently, Julie was finally able to coadopt Mak. The laws in New York regarding adoption have changed tremendously. Our case was pending for a long time. More and more queer parents are coadopting their partners' children now.

Have you discussed with the boys the issue of having two moms?

We've talked about it. They know that some people have two moms, and some have two dads, and some have a mom and a dad, and some have one mom and no dad, and some have a grandmother and no parents—all these things.

People think it's so confusing for kids, but it really isn't. It's very simple. The sheer variety of family structures in America today is something that seemingly no one—especially these conservative bigots who say we shouldn't have children—wants to acknowledge. But the facts are that the American family with two kids and the wife and husband, living alone in a little home without any help from anyone, no longer has validity. A *minority* of people in America live that way. The complexity of family life and interconnectedness is immense, and no one has really studied it. The arrangements people are making—not just queer people—to survive in this country's economic and social environment are extraordinary. If the academics weren't so blind to reality, this is what they'd be studying, because it's what is happening. It's old news to those of us who've been participating in it for years, but for some reason these people continue to hold on to some idea of the American family as being mom and dad and the kids in a station wagon. That's not real life.

How has it been with other families or schoolmates the boys are in contact with? Do they ever give them a hard time?
It's been fine. I've been an out dyke since I was in my twenties, and a published gay writer for years, so I'm not exactly hidden. And having children is a great leveler. The differences between queer people and straight people are actually significantly less when children are involved. Kids provide a terrific common ground. Both of our kids have special needs, so we spend a lot of time in doctors' offices and hospitals. And in *those* places, the differences among people are radically lessened. The nonsense falls away, and people are just human to one another. That's been an eye-opening experience. We are *all* human in the end, and we share more than we think. Our differences can be grotesquely unimportant, but knowing that in our hearts is what makes queer people different. And that's the conundrum of being queer: You understand the commonality of human experience in ways many straight people don't, because they've never had to think about it. At the same time, you are socially outside of things, included only in conditions of extremity.

For some gay people, having kids is about showing straight society that we can do it. Did you ever find that it worked the other way around, and that you

learned things about straight parents from having kids?

Absolutely. I will never again look at a harried mother on the street screaming at her kids and dragging them from one sidewalk to another and think that she's a horrible monster. Because now I know what it's like. I know exactly what she's going through. And when I see little kids crying and shrieking, I know what *they're* going through. It really has increased my understanding of the emotional truth and complexity of life and human existence. It's given me an understanding and comprehension far beyond anything I could have imagined, and it continues to teach me lessons of extraordinary love and courage, and sometimes of excruciating limitations.

With kids, your life really is no longer your own. You learn an acceptance of fate and a love of people and a respect of self that comes with it, as well as a giving up of self. It's a good training ground for life. It's really amazing.

Why do you think so many people are freaked out about queers adopting or having their own children?

Because it's different, plain and simple. Not in New York City maybe, or in San Francisco or a few other large cities. But in most places in our country, people are taught to be freaked out about change and difference. And unfortunately, growing up as one of those people means that you're constantly freaking out, because, more and more, everything in this country is changing.

Do you think young people are just as freaked out by it?
Human difference is really scary. One thing twelve-year-olds understand is that they don't want to be different, because other people will laugh at them. That's the main fear—that you'll be an outsider, a pariah. You don't want people to laugh, or point fingers at you, or walk up to you and ask hurtful questions—which kids do all the time. Mak has a cleft palate, and other children always ask him what his facial scars are, or why he talks funny. Van has some minor limb deformities, and they'll ask him questions about that. But my kids will have to get used to it. They're certainly in the right family for it, because I know what it's like to grow up different, and that will be a tremendous advantage for them.

For a twelve-year-old who thinks she might be queer and is worried about what people will think, the fear is very real. In America, we are taught that otherness is bad and sameness is good. Oh, we like to walk around with rings through our noses and say we're outsiders, but only if Madonna does it, too, or everyone else does it! We don't really like to be different.

My kids will have an edge growing up in an openly queer family, because they will come to see that human difference is a positive thing. No, it won't always be easy. But they'll get through it, and they have a lot of love. That's what's ultimately important.

To find out more about how gay people are forming families of their own, take a look at these books:

Getting Simon: Two Gay Doctors' Journey to Fatherhood (Bramble Books, 1995) by Kenneth B. Morgen. The story of two gay men's long struggle to adopt a child.

Lesbian and Gay Families: Redefining Parenting in America (Franklin Watts, 1995) by Jill S. Pollack. An easy-to-understand look at how lesbians and gay men are changing the way people look at what a family is.

Making Love Visible: In Celebration of Gay and Lesbian Families (The Crossing Press, 1995) by Geoff Manasse and Jean Swallow. This book combines text with beautiful photos depicting a wide range of lesbian and gay families.

LESBIAN AND GAY FAST FACT **EIGHT**

Don't Most Religions Say That Being Gay Is Wrong?

One of the most controversial topics in our society is about gay people and religion. Arguing about what different faiths say about homosexuality can fill up whole books, and many have been written about the subject. Different religions view gay people in different ways. Some groups, such as Buddhists and Quakers, have traditionally been very accepting of lesbian and gay people. Others, such as the Catholic church and the Baptist church, have generally viewed homosexuality as being unacceptable.

As our society changes, religious beliefs tend to change along with it. We've seen this in many areas. For a very long time, there were almost no women acting as ministers or rabbis. Now having women religious leaders is more common. Divorce used to be outlawed in many religious traditions, but now it is a much less controversial issue within many of them. In most religious groups, changes often occur when the needs of the members change. Something that makes sense at one time might not make sense later.

When it comes to accepting gay people, many churches have already changed their policies to some degree. The Episcopal church now allows the ordination of openly gay priests, and gay ministers can be found in many different churches, from Baptist to Lutheran. These people aren't always accepted by all the members of any given church, or by the governing body of their particular faith, but they are there. And many congregations are actively inviting lesbian and gay people into their families.

Religion should never be used as a weapon against anyone. Unfortunately, there are people who do use it as one. And because these people can often be very angry, it is easy to hate or fear them. Many gay and lesbian people have very negative feelings about religion because of what some religious people say about our community. And many gay people struggle to try not to be gay because their religion says it is wrong. What is important to remember is that a lot of the anger religious people have toward gay people is caused by just not understanding who we are. It takes time for people to change what they feel, and this includes religious people.

It is also important for gay people to know that

being gay doesn't have to mean not being religious. Many lesbian and gay people have active
lives in churches that accept gay people. Many others have fulfilling spiritual lives outside of established religious institutions. There are lots of ways
to be gay and still have a faith, if you want to.
Religion and spirituality aren't just for people who
follow a set of rules. They belong to all of us. Don't
let anyone tell you that you don't belong because
he or she doesn't like who you are.

RABBI LISA EDWARDS
SPIRITUAL LEADER

Religion plays an important role in the lives of many people. Unfortunately, in some instances religion has been used as a weapon against gay and lesbian people. Various religious organizations have claimed that homosexuality is against the teachings of the Bible and other religious documents. This argument is sometimes used to condone violence and discrimination toward gay people. More important, this intolerance on the part of some religious communities has caused many lesbian and gay people to think that there is no room in religion for them. They may leave the religious traditions they grew up with because they feel unwanted and unloved.

But more and more, gay people are now realizing that there is indeed room for us within the religions and spiritual traditions of the world. We are questioning the beliefs of people who say that gays and lesbians cannot be part of churches and synagogues. Sometimes we do this by forming our own churches, like the worldwide network of Metropolitan Community Churches that were established so that gay people could have a place to worship. Other times, we form gay and lesbian groups within already-

established traditions, such as Dignity, a group made up
of gay Catholics, and Integrity, a gay Episcopal group.

Gay religious organizations now include Buddhists,
Mormons, Baptists, Quakers, and other denominations.
Some of these groups are accepted and welcomed by their
traditions; others are not. In some traditions, we are see-
ing great changes because of the work these groups do,
such as the ordination of openly gay priests in the
Episcopal church, or the formation of gay-welcoming con-
gregations in historically antigay traditions like the
Baptist church.

Some of the most active lesbian and gay groups can be
found within the Jewish tradition. Lisa Edwards has
been the rabbi at Temple Beth Chayim Chadashim in Los
Angeles for three years. The congregation, which recently
celebrated its twenty-fifth anniversary, is the oldest les-
bian, gay, and bisexual synagogue in the world.

What was your childhood like?
I knew that I was a tomboy, and I was perfectly willing to be one. And my parents, for whatever reason, were also willing to let me be a tomboy. This
was during the fifties and sixties, when girls wearing pants was an odd thing, and they let me. So
they helped me to be comfortable with myself.
Being a tomboy back then was certainly not
unheard of, but it was unusual. Being a tomboy
doesn't mean you're a lesbian, but I know an awful
lot of lesbians who were.

Was your family religious?

My parents were married for a long time—sixteen years—before they had children. They were first-generation Americans. Both of them came from families that were assimilating into American culture at a pretty steady pace. So neither of my parents was very interested in Judaism until my brother and I came along. One of the reasons they weren't interested in Judaism was that there were things about many of the synagogues that they didn't like. So what they did was get a group of friends together and start their own. It started in someone's home. Now, all these years later, it's a large, mainstream Reform suburban congregation in Chicago.

Was there any discussion of homosexuality in your family?

No, I certainly don't remember any discussion about it. I remember riding in the car with my parents once when I was little—driving to the North Side of Chicago. And this pedestrian walked in front of the car when we were stopped at a light. And one of my parents said to the other, "Look at that." And when I asked what they were talking about, my mother said, "That's either a man trying to be a woman or a woman trying to be a man." And I couldn't see what they were talking about. It just looked like a regular person in a business suit to me.

Did you think about it a lot afterward?
I remember thinking that I liked the suit, and that I'd like to wear a suit like that someday.

Did you have any interest in being a rabbi then?
There had been remarks made at religious school one day that women could not be rabbis. I wasn't exactly a rebel as a kid, but I remember thinking that maybe I could be the first woman rabbi.

Were there any women rabbis as you got older?
The first woman rabbi was ordained in 1972, and I graduated from high school in 1970. But once there was a woman rabbi, then I didn't think much more about wanting to become one, because she'd done it. It wasn't until quite some time afterward that I thought about it again. My brother—who is four years older than I am—became a rabbi. And once he decided to do that, I really steered away from it, because all of my life I'd been the copycat little sister, and I wanted to get away from doing things because my brother did them.

Did you have lesbian feelings as you grew up?
I did, but I didn't recognize them for what they were. It's amazing how oblivious you can be to things. I knew that I was attracted to women, but it never occurred to me either to do anything about

that or that it meant anything. I had crushes on boys, too, and went to school dances and things when I could stand it. I didn't like the dresses you had to wear, though.

When did you come out?
Not until quite a bit later. I had a stint of being married to a man first.

Was that an attempt at getting away from being gay?
No, it was more just being oblivious to it. By that point, I think I was saying to myself, This must be what it means to be bisexual. There was this one woman I was in love with and would have liked to be sexual with, but she was straight, and there was no possibility of that. So I decided I must be bisexual. I no longer think that, but at the time it made sense to me.

What finally brought you out?
By then, I had that knowledge of what being lesbian was, but it wasn't a significant factor to me, because to me being monogamous meant that I had to stay with whomever I was with, which was my husband. Then I became less and less satisfied by the marriage, because I wasn't happy suppressing all my feelings. Then I met Tracy, who is still my partner. We became friends and fell in love. It just clicked. And once that happened, I realized that

this was what I'd always been and always would be. Everything fell into place.

Was it hard to end the marriage?
It was very hard. But I had to.

Did that coincide with your renewed interest in becoming a rabbi?
Those two things really blended. I came out—and I'd seen that it allowed me to start getting in touch with all the other pieces of my life I'd been ignoring while I tried to ignore my sexuality. By embracing that aspect of my life, I became a much more integrated person, because I was able to think about other things. When you hold back a piece of your life, or suppress it, it prevents you from really being your whole self.

I was in touch with the Jewish aspect of myself in a lot of ways. I still had a lot of interest in it. But by then, I'd gone back to school in Iowa, and there wasn't a large Jewish community there. There was only one synagogue, and because they had to be all things to all the Jewish people, they were very mainstream and very conservative. So I kept running into people like myself who you would think were just secular people with no interest in the religious aspects of being Jewish. But in fact, we were very interested in the religious part of our lives; we just didn't feel we belonged in that particular group. So we would meet together and study and socialize. And the more I did that, the more I realized that what I wanted was to take my spiritual life to the next step.

Were you concerned at that point about your lesbianism being a roadblock to becoming a rabbi?
The issue had not yet been addressed widely in the Jewish community, so I was concerned. I knew it would be coming up within the next few years in the Jewish Reform movement, which is one branch of Judaism. It had already come up in the Reconstructionist movement, so I applied first to their rabbinical school, because a policy of accepting gay and lesbian students had already been established.

So you were able to be open on your application?
I was. The problem was that Tracy was not Jewish. She has become Jewish since then, but she wasn't at the time. And there was not yet a policy regarding whether or not rabbinical students could be in relationships with non-Jewish partners. In fact, a policy was developed around my application, and it was decided that the partners of rabbinical students did have to be Jewish.

It's ironic that the thing you would expect to be an issue—being a lesbian—wasn't, and then you ran

into this other issue. Why is that?
I think the issue is about being models for the community. While the movement recognized that there are intermarriages within the community, and that it's here to stay, they don't think it's the model that should be presented to the community. There are students protesting it more and more, but all of the movements currently continue to hold that belief. Retaining a Jewish identity is perceived as being far more important than whether or not someone is gay or lesbian.

What did you do after being rejected there?
I applied to the Reform movement's rabbinical school. Because they hadn't yet made any rulings about accepting lesbian and gay students, I was only partly out to them. I was open in the psychological portion of my application, and the dean knew and a couple of other people on the admissions committee knew. They were fine about it. I don't think it was ever discussed. But I didn't put it in my application essay, and I didn't discuss it in my interview.

And you were accepted?
I was. The first year of the program was spent in Jerusalem, so Tracy and I left Iowa for Israel. Once I was actually there and in school, I didn't think

they would throw me out for being lesbian, so we
were very open as a couple.

What was the reaction?
It was mixed. There was never any threat to my status as a student, but then they did get distressed
about Tracy not being Jewish. And ultimately, she
studied and decided that conversion was the right
path for her, and she became Jewish.

Would she have done that if it wasn't an issue?
She would have. We discussed the issue with a lot
of people, and the opinion was that there were
enough battles to fight over being lesbian and a
rabbi, or a woman and a rabbi, and that adding
this one to it wouldn't do anyone any good. But
she wouldn't have done it if she hadn't felt it was
the right thing for her to do.

**Were you one of the first openly lesbian or gay
rabbis?**
I was one of the first to apply for jobs as an openly
lesbian rabbi. And I did feel I had trouble getting
jobs because of it. Which wasn't unexpected, of
course. And it's still true that it's hard, although
it's changing more and more as other gays and
lesbians are ordained. There are a lot more places
now that will consider taking on a gay or lesbian
rabbi. In fact, some of the places that said no to

me have since hired lesbians. And that's been only in the mid-1990s, so it shows a lot of progress.

Does that make you feel like a pioneer?
In a way. I mean, it was also an absolutely horrible experience for me. In some ways, it was powerful, but it was also terrible because there weren't huge numbers of people dealing with what I was dealing with. But there were enough gay and lesbian rabbis who were out before me, mostly at gay and lesbian synagogues, that I had some support. It wasn't as hard as it might have been had I been all alone. People had already paved the way.

You ended up in a gay/lesbian/bisexual congregation. Did you want to do that?
That's really what I wanted to do in the first place. When I went into rabbinical school, it was with the intention of working in that community.

So many gay and lesbian people abandon their faiths because they feel they aren't wanted there. What made you want to stay in yours?
It's more that their faiths abandon them. Every week, it seems we get someone stepping into the synagogue on Friday night who hasn't been there since their Bar Mitzvah or Bat Mitzvah. They thought they'd left it behind forever. And it's amazing to see people coming back to Judaism and feel-

ing comfortable. They either left it as kids because they weren't interested or they left it when they came out because they felt rejected by their families. Somehow they think Judaism was a complicating factor in their coming out. And with us, they find a community that tells them they can lead a Jewish life and be queer.

What did you connect with in your own faith that made you feel that this was what you wanted to do with your life?

When I was meeting with the Jewish group in Iowa, I was struck by how tentative we were about our Judaism. I felt that there was a lot more we could be doing with our faith, much more we could learn, and many more ways it could be applied to our lives. I have a passion about living a Jewish life, and part of living a Jewish life means not living in isolation. So that meant I had to find for myself or create for myself—as my parents had—a community in which I felt comfortable living, and where there were other people living a Jewish life along with me. And I think that's what we're doing. I love all the different pieces of what it means to be a rabbi in a community like this. I love helping people create life-cycle rituals—making transitions in their lives, mourning their losses, and celebrating the good things. To find within their traditions and their heritage a way to do that.

Do you do that by changing traditional services or language to include lesbian and gay people?
We do a lot of adaptation to make things inclusive. But none of it is unrecognizable. Any Jew could walk into our temple on any Friday night and feel at home. But there are enough differences that it allows all people to feel included in what we're doing.

What is the most rewarding thing for you about your work?
I think it's helping people figure out what Judaism can add to their lives. For example, a congregant recently lost her best friend. She had some background in Judaism but only fairly recently had returned to it. And she really had no idea what to do to mourn her loss. So we worked together, and I told her about the Jewish traditions of mourning, and we were able to create some rituals for her to remember her friend by and comfort her by reflecting on and telling stories about her friend. Those kinds of things are very rewarding to me.

What's the hardest part of your work?
All the death in our community from AIDS and cancer. Trying to figure out as a community how to deal with these losses. I think that's something we're still really struggling with.

Do you think that spiritual groups formed around common feelings—like a gay and lesbian temple—have stronger spiritual lives?

What I see in a congregation like ours—and gay and lesbian congregations in general—is that people come because they want to be here. Many synagogues these days have what people term "pediatric Judaism," meaning that it's centered around children, and not really the spiritual lives of adults. Our congregation is different. People come because they want to be there, because they're excited about being Jewish. And now, happily, we're getting to the point where many of our members are having children or planning on having children. So there will be this new dimension to the community. That will be wonderful.

Do you think lesbian and gay people have a deeper understanding of why spirituality is important to them, because so many have been rejected by their traditions?

Some do, but not necessarily. I think what I see over and over again is that there are people in their thirties or forties who are fairly successful and have been out in the world for a while, and they're coming back because they're looking for something more in their lives.

Do you find young people coming in?

We're getting more and more, and now we do more outreach to those groups. If young people have grown up in a liberal Jewish community, there has often been at least lip service paid to the idea that there are gays, lesbians, and bisexuals in the community. I recently went to talk to a confirmation group, and the kids said, "Why do they keep sending people to talk to us about gays and lesbians? What's the big deal? We know gay people." So those kinds of kids know. But there are still a lot who don't ever hear that gays and lesbians are welcome. As teenagers, it's tricky to know about yourself or be out enough to search for your own synagogue. We have one very active sixteen-year-old whose mother brought her to us because she needed support. And it turned out that her father—the parents were divorced—was also gay, so the two of them started coming together. And that was great to see.

I can't even imagine someone doing that when I was sixteen.
I can't, either. If the words *gay* or *lesbian* were ever spoken, it was as a put-down. It just wasn't talked about.

A lot of gay people think we should abandon traditional religion because of its intolerance and form

**our own ways of worshiping. What do you think
about that?**

I think we don't have to invent our own spirituality.
It's fine if you can, but people should know that
there is spirituality that exists already, and that we
fit into those traditions. It's hard for people to see
that sometimes. A lot of people say to me, "But
doesn't the Torah say this is wrong?" And I say,
"Well, yes, it does. But the Torah says many things
that we understand differently now." People forget
that so much of what we call "religion" is someone's interpretation of what spirituality should be.
We can find ways to remain in our traditions and
still make them ours.

**Do people ever give you a hard time about staying
inside the traditional faith?**

Yes, although I get that less and less. I got a lot of
it when I first started. Some radical feminists wonder how I can stay within a patriarchal, misogynist
religion. Again, I think that's about how people
interpret it. Those discriminations aren't actually
at the core of the faith. God is for everyone equal-
ly, and the core of Judaism is justice.

Is your life what you expected it to be?

A lot of it is better than I expected. I think the
peace of being true to who you are and going with

what makes sense to you and what you can feel and reason are the important things. That's what I see over and over again in my life. Once I got in touch with what I felt and was true to that, my life became so much more rewarding. And I see that in others, as well. People are looking for ways to live their lives that allow them to do what they think is right. It's always amazing to me how good people are.

Would you want to work in a straight congregation?
Not really. When I go to other congregations, it's not that they're alien to me exactly, but it's just not family in the same way that my congregation is. One idea that bothers me—as with this whole thing about gay marriage—is the idea that gays and lesbians are just like everyone else. We aren't like everyone else. I do think we deserve the same rights, but I think we are very different in many important ways. And those things should be celebrated. We should rejoice in that and accept those differences, enjoy them.

GAY AND LESBIAN SPIRITUALITY

Homosexuality is a much-debated topic in many of the world's established religions. Some religions are welcoming and supportive of lesbians and gays. Others find homosexuality completely unacceptable. Many fall somewhere in between. Whatever religion you are or are interested in knowing more about, you can probably find a group of gay and lesbian people who are living within the same tradition. Sometimes these groups are recognized by the larger church, but often they are not.

The following list gives information on how to contact some of the most active gay and lesbian religious groups. The addresses and telephone numbers provided are for each group's main office. However, it is very possible that there are branches of the groups in or near your own town. This is especially true of large groups such as Dignity (gay Catholics) and Integrity (gay Episcopalians). Before calling the main offices, check the white pages of the telephone directory to see if there is a local chapter of the group you are interested in. You might also want to call your local gay and lesbian community center to see if any groups meet there. If you can't find any information that way, call or write to these organizations and ask for a list of groups that meet in your area.

Some of the organizations listed have Web sites on the World Wide Web. Often these sites will contain links to other sites. If you're interested in finding out more about how various religious traditions view homosexuality, or in learning about how gays and lesbians in various religious groups are working to bring about changes for gay people in those groups, then these Web sites can be very informative and useful ways to get information.

If you don't see a listing here for a group you're interested in, don't give up. Some groups simply do not have national headquarters or organized member lists, but instead hold small local meetings that might be advertised in local gay newspapers or at community centers. This is especially true for very strict religious groups such as Muslims or Hindus, who for various reasons (primarily because homosexuality is considered a great taboo) do not have organized lesbian and gay religious movements. If you are a member of one of these religions, you might have a harder time finding lesbian and gay groups. But if you look around, you'll probably find some. On-line computer "chat" boards associated with particular religions are also good ways to find gay and lesbian groups.

Other groups, particularly Buddhists, are almost always welcoming of gay and lesbian people, and many gay groups exist around the country. If you are interested in gay Buddhist groups, look in the yellow pages of the telephone book under *Buddhism* or *Meditation Centers* and call a few places to ask if they have groups specifically for lesbians and gay men. Even if they don't, chances are they would be happy to see you anyway. Gay Jewish groups are also many and varied, and they differ from city to city. The best way to find a gay Jewish group or temple is to look in your local gay newspaper or to call the nearest lesbian and gay community center or Jewish community center.

One religious group unique to the gay and lesbian community is the Metropolitan Community Church, often called just MCC. A nondenominational church, the MCC has branches in many different cities—both large and small—across the world. To see if there is an MCC branch in your area, look in the white pages of the telephone book under *Metropolitan Community Church.*

Affirmation (Mormons)
P.O. Box 46022
Los Angeles, CA 90046-0022
Phone: (213) 255-7251
World Wide Web: www.affirmation.org

Affirmation (United Methodists)
P.O. Box 1021
Evanston, IL 60204
Phone: (847) 733-9590
E-mail: umaffirm@concentric.net
World Wide Web: www.umaffirm.org

Association of Welcoming and Affirming Baptists
P.O. Box 2596
Attleboro Falls, MA 02763-0894
Phone: (508) 226-1945
E-mail: wabaptists@aol.com

Axios: Eastern and Orthodox Christian Gay Men
and Women
P.O. Box 990
Village Station
New York, NY 10014-0704
Phone: (212) 989-6211
E-mail: axiosusa@aol.com

Brethren/Mennonite Council for Lesbian and
Gay Concerns
P.O. Box 6300
Minneapolis, MN 55406-0300
Phone: (612) 722-6906
E-mail: bmc@webcom.com
World Wide Web: www.webcom.com/bmc

Dignity (Catholics)
National Office
1500 Massachusetts Avenue NW, Suite 11
Washington, DC 20005
Phone: (202) 861-0017
Toll-free phone: (800) 877-8797
E-mail: dignity@aol.com
World Wide Web: www.dignityusa.org

Emergence International (Christian Scientists)
P.O. Box 6061-423
Sherman Oaks, CA 91413
Phone: (818) 994-6653
Toll-free phone: (800) 280-6653
E-mail: billxls@aol.com

Evangelical Network (Evangelical Christian)
P.O. Box 16104
Phoenix, AZ 85011-6104
E-mail: evangelnet@aol.com

Friends for Lesbian and Gay Concerns (Quakers)
143 Campbell Avenue
Ithaca, NY 14850

Integrity (Episcopalians)
P.O. Box 5255
New York, NY 10185-5255
Phone: (212) 691-7181

Interweave (Unitarian Universalists)
167 Milk Street, #406
Boston, MA 02109
E-mail: alan@spdcc.com

Kinship International (Seventh-Day Adventists)
P.O. Box 7320
Laguna Niguel, CA 92607
Phone: (714) 248-1299
E-mail: sdakinship@aol.com

Lutherans Concerned
E-mail: luthconc@aol.com
World Wide Web: www.lcna.org

Reconciling Congregation Program (Methodists)
3801 N. Keeler Avenue
Chicago, IL 60641
Phone: (773) 736-5526

United Fellowship of Metropolitan Community
Churches (nondenominational)
8714 Santa Monica Boulevard, 2nd Floor
West Hollywood, CA 90069
Phone: (310) 360-8640
E-mail: ufmcchq@aol.com
World Wide Web: www.ufmcc.com

World Congress of Gay and Lesbian Jewish
Organizations
P.O. Box 23379
Washington, DC 20026-3379
World Wide Web: www.wcgljo.org/wcglo/

LESBIAN AND GAY FAST FACT **NINE**

What Does "Coming Out" Mean?

The term *coming out* means being open about being a lesbian or gay person. It's really a shortened version of the phrase "coming out of the closet." If someone is not open about being lesbian or gay, we say the person is "in the closet," or "closeted."

All of the people whose stories are included in this book have come out. They all live as openly gay or lesbian people. But not all gay people come out. For many reasons, some women and men choose never to reveal their gay identities. The choice of whether or not to come out is up to each individual.

A lot of people think that coming out means you run up and down the street telling everyone you see that you're gay. While it can mean this, for most of us it is not quite that dramatic. In fact, it is generally an ongoing process that takes us our whole lives. It's a series of steps we take one at a time.

Coming out begins with ourselves. It means accepting that we are gay or lesbian and accepting that this is a special part of who we are as people. That's the first step. From there, coming out takes many forms. It might mean telling a friend or a family member. It might mean going to a meeting of a gay and lesbian support group. It could be telling a teacher. All of these things are ways of coming out.

The idea of coming out frightens many gay people, because it means facing what other people might think about us. It can seem like an overwhelming task to tell all the people in our lives that we're gay. That is why it is a good idea to think of it as something you can do gradually. Start by coming out to yourself. Then, when you think you're ready, consider coming out in other ways.

Coming out has special concerns for young people. In some ways, it can be a great thing. Being out means that you can more easily involve yourself with your local gay community. It also means that you can be a role model to other young people who might not be out yet. But there can also be drawbacks. While we all have to deal with what our families think when we come out, it is much harder to do when you are still living at home. And while things have gotten easier for gay young people, it is still difficult to be an openly gay person in any school.

If you are a gay young person thinking about coming out, consider it carefully. It is a very brave, important, and far-reaching thing to do, and you want to make sure you will have a support network to help you deal with whatever happens. And remember that you don't have to come out if you are not ready to, or if you are in a situation where doing so isn't safe for you. Part of taking care of yourself as a lesbian or gay person means knowing when it is best for you to share who you are with other people.

KEVIN JENNINGS
EDUCATOR

One of the most controversial topics surrounding the gay community is what young people should be taught about lesbians and gays. All across the country, communities are debating what children should learn in school about gay people, and whether or not gay issues are appropriate for discussion in classrooms. In some places, school boards have decided that students cannot learn about gay people in their districts. In others, teaching respect for lesbian and gay people and learning about gay issues have become part of the curriculum.

Caught in the middle of these debates are the teachers, who can get into trouble if they go against their schools' policies regarding discussing gay issues in class. Things are especially difficult for gay and lesbian teachers. While many gay teachers want to come out, others are afraid that if they do, they will lose their job or be accused of trying to "recruit" their students to a gay lifestyle.

Also affected by these issues are gay and lesbian students, many of whom have nowhere to turn for support and guidance. While many schools across the country now have very active gay student groups, many more do not. And in some school districts, antigay opponents are trying to make sure that gay student groups are never formed there.

The leading voice in the fight for the rights of gay teachers and gay students is Kevin Jennings. One of the first educators to come out and publicly demand respect for gay people—both students and teachers—he has been responsible for bringing about many changes in the way schools address gay issues. He is the founder and executive director of GLSEN—the Gay, Lesbian, Straight Education Network—and is also the author of the books One Teacher in Ten: Gay and Lesbian Educators Tell Their Stories; Becoming Visible: A Reader in Gay and Lesbian History for High School and College Students; *and* Telling Tales Out of School: Lesbian, Gay, and Bisexual People Remember Their School Years.

What was life like for you growing up?
I grew up in rural North Carolina. Starting in sixth grade, I was labeled "the school fag," and I had a really horrible school experience from then on. I had several years where I ate every school meal alone. I was called names. I was beaten up a couple of times, and I had one of my teeth knocked out and my hand broken. It was really nightmarish.

How did this affect you?
I tried to kill myself as a teenager, and I developed

a real substance-abuse problem because of it all. I also came from a very poor family. My father, who had been a traveling Southern Baptist preacher, died when I was eight. My mother, who had only a junior high school education, had to support the family, and the only job she could get was working at McDonald's. We lived in a trailer for most of my life. And my mother always emphasized that the way out of this kind of life was to get an education. So school was both a place of torture for me and the place where I had the most success. I was the only one of my sixty-four cousins, and the only one of the five kids in my immediate family, who got to go to college. I went to Harvard.

Why did you decide to become a teacher?

When I graduated from college, I knew that I wanted to make a difference in the world. As a kid, I was taught that there were always people who were less fortunate than we were. No matter how poor you are, there's always someone poorer. My mother always coordinated the Christmas charity drive, and she always reminded us that there were people worse off than we were, and that the most important thing we could do in life was help those people.

I had wanted to go into politics, but having come out of the closet in college, I thought that was now out of the question. I also believed that I could make a bigger difference working with young people, because by the time people are grown up, they've mostly made up their minds about things. I thought the best way to change the world would be by becoming a teacher.

Were you out at your teaching job?
The first job I had was a very negative experience. I was told that if I came out, I would be fired. After two years of remaining closeted, I couldn't stand it anymore. I'd always been taught not to lie, and I felt as though hiding who I was as a person was lying. So I left that school and went to another one.

Was that better?
I wore a wedding ring at that time, because my first partner and I had exchanged rings. The kids started to ask me questions about it. I decided that I was going to answer the questions honestly, and I did.

What was the reaction?
A very interesting thing started to happen. The kids somehow thought that I had told them something bad about myself, and that they should keep it a secret. So they didn't tell anyone else, and that's not what I wanted. I wanted them to understand that being gay wasn't something to be ashamed of.

How did you help them understand that?

I ended up giving a speech to the entire school, in which I came out.

What did that feel like?

I was absolutely terrified. I was convinced that I was going to lose my job. More important, I was afraid that the kids would turn on me. Because after all, when I was a kid and the other kids thought I was gay, they attacked me. I thought the same thing would happen again.

And did that happen?

Just the opposite. When I finished speaking, kids swarmed the stage and hugged me and told me how proud they were of me. I felt like a celebrity or something.

How did things change for you after that?

Suddenly, I found myself being the expert on gay teachers. I was asked to write an article about it for a magazine, because I was the only out teacher they could find. This was in 1988, and at that time gay teachers just did not come out publicly.

Why not?

It was very hard for teachers to come out of the closet, because they would be accused of trying to recruit children to the gay lifestyle or of promoting

homosexuality. Teaching is one of the most difficult professions for gay people—right up there
with the military. At that time, there weren't very
many of us who were out. And all of a sudden, people started contacting me and asking me to orga-
nize conferences and write articles and do other
things centered around the issues of gay teachers
and students. I quickly realized that there needed
to be an organization for gay educators. So in
1990, along with a lesbian teacher, I started what
was then called the Gay, Lesbian, and Straight
Teachers Network.

What did the GLSTN do?
We did not want to be a teachers' support group,
because we didn't feel that would accomplish anything in terms of changing attitudes toward gay
teachers. We felt that what would really be useful to
gay teachers is if we could work to get rid of homophobia. The mistake I'd seen many groups make
was that they ended up just being a support group
where people sat around and talked about how miserable they were. We didn't think that would
change anything. So we decided to advocate for
change in the way that schools dealt with gay issues.

Did that work?
We were wonderfully successful. We got the state of
Massachusetts, where we were located, to add sex-

ual orientation as a protected class to the Equal
Education law.

What did that mean?

It meant that, essentially, they banned antigay bias
in schools. Now one out of every three public high
schools in Massachusetts has a gay-straight alliance.
It means that any student who is called names or
discriminated against has the law on his or her side.
We designed a program called Safe Schools for Gay
and Lesbian Students to help schools comply with
the law by doing things such as training their teachers and setting up gay-straight alliances in schools.

**How does antigay behavior affect straight stu-
dents?**

The really interesting thing to me is that part of
the reason I was labeled a "fag" was because I was a
smart boy. The message then was that boys were
not supposed to be smart. They weren't supposed
to raise their hands in class or do their homework
or cooperate with teachers. I did those things
because my mother made it clear that learning and
getting an education was the only way out of poverty.

One of the things I try to get across when I work
with schools is that antigay behavior affects more
than just gay kids. It's a way of enforcing negative
social norms, and of stigmatizing and hurting kids
in many ways. The message being sent to boys is

that if you're smart, or if you display an interest in learning, you're not one of the crowd, and that often translates into being called a "fag," because it's the worst name people can think of to call you.

What that does is equate being gay with being an outsider. I attribute a large part of the ignorance in schools to homophobia, because kids are fearful of being perceived as being different, even when they aren't actually gay. Teachers have to challenge bigotry in all its forms, because bigotry is a way of making people act in ways that are not who they are.

How did GLSTN grow to become a nationwide organization?

I wrote a book called *One Teacher in Ten*, which is a collection of essays by lesbian and gay teachers. I met a lot of people while working on the book. I was also getting calls from people from all over the country, asking me how they could do in their states what we had done in Massachusetts. It was very clear to me that there needed to be a national organization. So in 1994, I left my job, before we'd even raised a single penny, and became the first employee of the nationwide GLSTN.

Was it difficult to get the organization going?

The first year, I would literally call up people in different areas and ask if they needed someone to come speak about this issue there. I just kept doing that, going all over the country, sleeping on people's couches and talking to people who would listen, just to get the message out. And by doing that, I found a lot of other people who were interested in this issue. Now we have over sixty chapters and six full-time staff people. We are the second-largest chapter-based organization in the gay movement. We've also changed our name to the Gay, Lesbian, and Straight Education Network to reflect the fact that our members come from many different parts of the education field.

What other gains have you made?
Well, recently I met with President Clinton as part of a group of people from the gay community who went to the White House to discuss gay issues. I talked with him about the issues faced by gay students. A few years ago, I was sleeping on couches while trying to get my message out. Now GLSEN is on the shortlist of organizations asked to advise the President on gay issues. That's a big accomplishment, and I'm very proud of it. I feel as though I've made a big contribution to making the lives of the next generation better.

Does it make you feel like a part of gay history?
I look at life as a chain. My ability to have the level of freedom that I have was made possible because the generation of gay people before me took

incredible risks and made incredible sacrifices—sometimes literally sacrificing their lives—in order to win some measure of freedom. I feel that my responsibility is to continue that process, to make sure that the generation after me is a little freer than I am. I really see myself carrying on that legacy, and I'm very grateful to the people who made my life possible.

Were there specific experiences with gay students that affected you and made you want to help more people?

My very first openly gay student came into my office one day. He was having unprotected sex a lot, and I was very disturbed by that. But when I told him that he had to practice safer sex, I will never forget his response. He said, "Why should I use a condom? My life isn't worth saving anyway." I really vowed, because of that student, that the goal of GLSEN would be that no student ever feels that way again, that no kid ever feels that his or her life is worth less than someone else's just because he or she is gay. And also that no straight student feels that another person's life is less important because she or he is gay.

What about your own life as a young person—when were you aware that you were gay?

I knew at about age seven or eight.

What were your feelings about gay people?
I grew up in the Baptist church, so I had very strong beliefs that gay people went to hell, because that's what I was taught. Furthermore, I was told that if you *thought* you wanted to do these things, that was as bad as actually doing them. It was made very clear to me that God wrote down every single sin you committed, including the ones you only thought about, and that when you died, God would read them all back to you. We were also taught that dead people knew everything you were thinking, so since my father died when I was eight, I thought that he was watching me from heaven, knowing everything I did.

Did you think there were other gay people around you?
Not at all. I thought gay people were from very far away, in places like San Francisco. They were not from my community. As far as I knew, there were none anywhere that I knew of.

What made even more of an impact on me was history. I became a history teacher because my mother taught me a lot of history when I was growing up. And knowing about history gave me a real sense of fitting into something larger than myself. But I never saw gay people in that history. It seemed to me that gay people were some kind of freaks from outer space, because there simply was no mention of them in the history books, so I didn't know where they came from. Later, I wrote a gay history book for high school kids, because I think knowing your history is a very big part of feeling proud of yourself.

Did you have bad impressions of what gay people were like from the people around you?
I definitely heard negative things from other kids. I remember once at school, when I was in ninth grade, there was a big debate over the Equal Rights Amendment, which would have changed the Constitution to ban discrimination on the basis of gender. And I spoke up for it, and one of the other kids said, "Oh, are you for a gay rights amendment, too?" And I said, "I don't believe that people should be discriminated against for any reasons," which, of course, was not the best answer to give. People laughed and tortured me for weeks for saying that. So the message that being gay was bad was delivered very clearly to me in many ways.

Did you look for mentions of gay people in books in the library?
Yes, I did all that. And of course I didn't find anything. Years later, when I was doing research for my own book, I was reading through an issue of *One* magazine, which was America's first gay magazine,

published in the 1950s. And there in the "Letters to the Editor" section, I saw a letter that was written by someone from Winston-Salem, North Carolina, which was my hometown. This letter was written by a gay person living in my town ten years before I was born, and I thought about how my life might have been different if I'd known about that, if I'd had this history about people like me. I think if I had known that there were people fighting for gay rights when I was a kid, my life would have been very different.

When did you finally come out to yourself?
It was really an ongoing process. When I was in high school, I definitely knew I was gay, but I didn't want to accept that. I would have sexual experiences with other boys, but I always told myself that they were gay and I wasn't. Then, when I was seventeen, I had a sexual experience with another boy where I actively pursued him, and that made me so upset that I tried to kill myself, because it was the first time I had to admit that I wanted another man sexually.

What were you thinking at that time?
I remember thinking that I had tried so hard to get rid of these feelings and had failed. It was like hanging on to a cliff by my fingernails. I'd held on so long—denying the truth—that my fingers had

slipped, and I didn't care to try to grab on again. I just wanted to fall.

What stopped you from actually doing it?
I tried taking an overdose of aspirin, but all it did was make me sick for days. My mother didn't even know I'd tried it. She just thought I had stomach flu.

What was it like going to college at a big school like Harvard, where there was an entirely different atmosphere from the one in your small town?
Before I left for school, I got this mailing from the school listing all of the clubs I could join. And one of them was a gay student organization. I remember being horrified, and wondering if I was the only one they'd sent it to or if they somehow knew I was gay. But I was also very excited to know it was there.

I didn't come out until my sophomore year. When I did, I came out in a very prominent way, and I became very involved with gay issues. I was very vocal about gay issues, and when I graduated, in 1985, I was one of two students chosen by my class to speak at the commencement ceremonies, where part of my speech dealt with homophobia.

What caused you to come out there?
My sophomore year, there was a guy I was very attracted to, and I knew he was gay. I remember

one day seeing him sitting in the dining room eating his breakfast, and all I could think was, Oh, my God, there's a homosexual sitting in here eating breakfast. And he didn't seem traumatized. He didn't seem scared. He was just eating cereal. That had a big impact on me, because he made being gay seem so normal.

The other thing was that I had a tutor in my dorm. We became friends, and one night I was in his room and picked up a newspaper. I realized that it was a gay paper, and I freaked out. He asked me if I had ever read it, and I wondered why he thought I would be reading a gay paper. I didn't know what to say, and finally I just said, "I think I might be gay." He was the first person I ever really told.

It was those things, basically—seeing that gay people did things like eat breakfast and read newspapers—that made me understand that it was normal to be this way.

Did you tell your family?

I came out to my mother, and she had a really hard time for a few years. We essentially had a "don't ask, don't tell" policy about it. We never talked about it. Both of us were too scared to do what we needed to do. I was too scared to tell her how much keeping things inside hurt me. And she was too scared to ask any questions, because she didn't want to hurt me. It really wasn't until a few years ago, when I started to do the work with GLSEN, that we sat down and actually discussed these things. And now she's a huge fan of what I do. She started the first chapter of Parents and Friends of Lesbians and Gays in North Carolina. She's so proud of me.

And that gives me a huge amount of hope for other people. My mother is in her seventies. She grew up in the hills of eastern Tennessee. Her family was unbelievably poor and had very little education. So she's exactly the kind of person you would expect not to be accepting of gay people. But she has learned about the issues, and she understands why fighting for these things is important. That's a real inspiration to me in the work I do, because it shows how people can change if we take the time to educate them.

Do you really think that people who are antigay can change?
I think it's our obligation as a community and as a movement to reach out to the people who don't understand, and to help them change. I really don't think that people by nature are mean or unjust. I think people are unjust or cruel out of ignorance, fear, and misinformation. I don't think there are lots of bad people; I think that lots of good people are encouraged to do bad things. I see my mission in life as trying to encourage peo-

ple to rise to the best of themselves instead of sinking to the lowest of themselves.

Do you think it's important for people to come out to their parents?

Yes, although my advice to young people thinking about coming out is to make a very real assessment of what the risks and repercussions are for them. I know a lot of young people who have come out and been hurt in some way by their parents.

However, I also think that we project a lot of fear about coming out. There are lots of young people who come out, and it's no big deal. Many times parents are ready to accept us as gay people long before we're ready to let them do it. So you have to make an honest evaluation of what might happen if you come out. How much of your fear is based on external realities and how much stems from projecting your own fears and self-loathing onto others? That's what you have to determine by truly and honestly assessing the environment. People are generally not as bad as we think they are.

When you first started teaching, what kind of fears were there for gay teachers?

It was absurd. The whole notion of coming out as a gay teacher in 1985, when I started my first job, was not even thought about. It wasn't even questioned. It was just assumed that if you did, you would be accused of all kinds of things, from child molestation to promoting a gay agenda.

How did that affect you as a gay teacher?
It was very hard, because I had no role models to look up to. I had no one who had done it before me to talk to.

Were people afraid because teachers had been fired for coming out, or because there were actually laws that affected gay teachers?
It was mostly imaginary fear. I have found that for the vast majority of teachers who come out, things are just fine. But people expect to be rejected for being gay, so they ignore all of the positive evidence around them and dwell on the one or two negative stories they've heard about teachers who came out and were fired.

This isn't to say that bad things don't happen. Some teachers have been fired. But not as widely as the fear of coming out suggests.

Are there any actual laws saying a gay or lesbian person can't be a teacher?
No, but there are also no laws, at least in thirty-nine states, that protect gay teachers from being fired. There have been some very highly publicized witch-hunts for gay teachers—most notably, the Save Our Children campaign headed by Anita

Bryant in the 1970s—which have made gay teachers very fearful of coming out. Because teachers work with young people, we are the number-one target of groups who think that homosexuals recruit children into being gay or lesbian.

When you were thinking of becoming a teacher, did you think you couldn't because you were gay?
Absolutely. But at the time, I thought I would be able to keep my private and public lives separate. I had no intention at the time of becoming this advocate for gay teachers. I never thought I'd be doing what I'm doing now.

Do you think you can come out as a gay person and not get involved in the gay community?
Not if you have a conscience. When you are gay and you come out, if you look around you all that you can see are opportunities where you can make a difference and places that need your help. Caring and thoughtful people are automatically going to get involved. It doesn't mean you plan to do this. I had no intention of doing this. But then I saw the needs that were out there, and I knew I had to respond to them.

Why do you think it's important for gay teachers to come out?
Young people learn their sets of values from two

main groups of people—their parents and their teachers. So if children grow up with gay teachers who are positive influences in their lives, then when they hear antigay statements, they are going to know that they aren't true.

That's why antigay politicians are so upset about gay teachers. They know that they can't win elections if everyone who ever had a gay teacher or any other positive gay role model in their lives doesn't vote for them.

Do you ever think it's all too hard and too much to do?
When I started out, I thought that if I just spoke out passionately and told the truth, people would realize they were wrong. Now I understand that creating change is a slower, more complicated process that takes time and patience. We just have to make sure it keeps going forward. I know that one day we will win the fight against homophobia. I have no doubt about that. I would like it to be in my lifetime, but even if it doesn't happen in mine, that's okay, because I know that it will eventually and that I'm doing something to make it happen.

What is your advice to gay and lesbian students who might want to get the people in their schools talking about gay issues?

The most important step to take is to empower yourself. The real battle for gay people is not winning an election or getting a policy passed. It's the battle for visibility. So the minute you speak out for your rights, you've won a major part of the battle. The biggest barriers to freedom lie within ourselves, and those are keeping silent because of our fears of being rejected and the way we accept limitations on our freedoms. When we stop being afraid and start speaking out, then we take giant steps forward. Even if you don't see change happening around you, it is happening. Just by being visible, you are making changes that can never be reversed.

If you are interested in starting a gay-straight alliance at your school, you can find help getting started with the Gay, Lesbian, and Straight Education Network's booklet *Starting a Gay-Straight Alliance*. The booklet can be ordered by writing or calling GLSEN, or it can be downloaded from GLSEN's Web site. The GLSEN Web site also provides information on many different subjects of importance to lesbian and gay students and educators. In addition, it includes an extensive resource section for those interested in the issues surrounding gay educators, in reaching lesbian and gay students, and in impacting legislation that affects these groups.

Gay, Lesbian, and Straight Education Network (GLSEN)
121 West 27th Street, Suite 804
New York, NY 10001
Phone: (212) 727-0135
World Wide Web: www.glsen.org

LESBIAN AND GAY FAST FACT **TEN**

I Want to Come Out, But How Do I Do It?

If you have decided that you are at a point in your life where you are ready to come out, the next step is deciding how to do it. The quickest way is just to tell people. If you decide to do this, it's best to pick a quiet, relaxed time. Coming out ten minutes before Thanksgiving dinner or while you and your best friend are rushing out the door to go to a movie is probably not a good idea. Choose a time when you know you will have awhile to discuss any questions that might come up.

It is never a good idea to come out in an attempt to hurt or get even with someone. Coming out should be something that you have thought about carefully and decided to do because it is the natural next step in your life, not something you do because you feel you have to do it, because someone else says you have to do it, or because you want to shock people.

When coming out in person, the important thing is to say what you want to in a simple, honest way.

You might say, "I've always shared a lot with you, and there's something I'd like to tell you that you might not know," or "I've been doing a lot of thinking about myself over the last few months and want to share with you some of the things I've learned." What you say and how you say it are up to you. What's most important is that you try to keep the conversation open and honest. It's very hard to tell people personal things about ourselves. Telling a friend, or your father or mother, that you are gay is an incredibly big step. You can make it a lot easier for yourself and for others if you are willing to discuss things.

Another way to come out to people is by letter. Telling someone this way can be easier, because it gives the other person time to think about things before seeing you or speaking to you. Writing a letter also gives you a lot of time to decide what you want to say.

However you decide to come out, you have to prepare yourself for different kinds of reactions. You might find that you have to answer a lot of questions and help people understand what you are telling them. How can you do this? You can be honest and answer their questions—even the ones that sound silly to you—as well as you can. Strange as it may seem, you may have to educate your friends and family about what being gay means. It may take them a long time to be able to talk to you about it.

If you are interested in coming out and what might lie ahead for you as an out gay person, you might want to take a look at these books. Both of them address a variety of issues important to lesbian and gay young people, including what to expect after you come out, finding a gay community around you, and dealing with issues such as sex, self-esteem, homophobia, and spirituality. They also include interviews with people from the gay and lesbian community.

Free Your Mind: The Book for Gay, Lesbian, Bisexual Youth—and Their Allies (HarperCollins, 1996) by Ellen Bass and Kate Kaufman.

The World Out There: Becoming Part of the Lesbian and Gay Community (The New Press, 1996) by Michael Thomas Ford.

TIM GILL
BUSINESS EXECUTIVE

In the world of computers, the name Quark is a giant. Their product Quark XPress is the most widely used electronic publishing software in the world. What many people might not know is that the cofounder of the company, Tim Gill, is an out gay man. Because the business world is not as flashy as the film or music industries, we don't often think about the impact that lesbians and gay businesspeople can have. But as Tim Gill has shown, people who are willing to be out gay people in the everyday world of business can often make just as great an impact as those who might be more visible. He is also an excellent example of the way many lesbian and gay people are using their professional interests to support the gay community.

Did you know you were gay as a young person?
In a lot of ways, I was kind of oblivious to the whole social scene. In a sense, being gay didn't bother me at all until sometime in late junior high or early high school, when I found out that there was this word—*homosexual*—and that I was one of those, and that that was a bad thing to be. Up until then,

it didn't bother me, because I really didn't know. I knew I liked guys, but that didn't seem like a bad thing to me. It wasn't until I put a name to it. And then I went on the usual guilt trip so many of us go on. It wasn't too terribly severe until right before I went to college.

What happened then?
The college sent me a school newspaper, and I was looking through it and saw an ad for Boulder Gay Liberation. They were going to have a camp-out, and I thought, Oh my God, there are other people like me in Colorado. I kind of knew that there were gay people in New York, because I had seen something about it in *Life* magazine. But I didn't think there were any in Denver, where I lived. So I was very excited, and I tried to think of ways that I could go to the camp-out. Then I realized that the paper was from the beginning of the summer, and I'd already missed it. I was distraught. But at least I knew there were other gay people. And probably the second day I was in college, I went into the office of Boulder Gay Liberation, and the first thing I said was, "Hi," and the second was, "Hello," and then I just shook for about ten minutes. And the guy who was there talked to me and calmed me down. And that was really the only negative thing that happened to me in coming out. Because after that initial ten minutes of terror, I was fine.

Did you have any preconceptions of what gay people were like?

No, I didn't. I guess I kind of knew that gay people were supposed to be effeminate, but this wasn't a very strong perception—mostly because I tend not to believe things I hear about other people. I wait until I meet them myself and then make my own judgments. My parents were wonderful about that. Not that they said it was okay to be gay, but they taught me that you have to have respect for other people, and that other people can be different from you and that's okay.

Did you tell them about yourself right away?

That depends on your definition of "right away." I came out in early September of 1972 and told them in December. I told all of my close friends within a week or two. I think I told my sisters before I told my parents. My parents were the last ones to know.

They usually are. What did they say?

What they said was very odd. They said, "Well, we knew that when you went to college you'd be more susceptible to that kind of thing." And they took me to see a psychiatrist the next day. This was in 1972, and I think that was right around the time that they removed homosexuality from the list of psychiatric disorders. And the psychiatrist said,

"Well, if you want to change, I will help you. Otherwise, we just have to work on your parents." I told him I didn't want to change, so we worked on my parents. And my mother went through the whole "where did I go wrong" stuff that so many parents seem to, and she started reading all of these pop-psychology books. Eventually, she got so into psychology that she decided to go back to school and she got a master's degree in psychology and a teaching certificate. So I blame myself that she has her master's degree.

That's a great ending to the story.
Compared with stories of parents who disown their children, it went fairly smoothly. But it really took them a couple of years to adjust. Essentially, by the time I was in my junior year of college, they had accepted that I was going to be gay. I had a boyfriend at the time, and they let me borrow their sports car for our first anniversary. And now my parents and my boyfriend's parents spend time together. We all spend Christmas together. Davol and I have been together for ten years, so I have the longest relationship of all my siblings.

You came out at an interesting time. The Stonewall riots were in 1969, and that was the start of the modern gay rights movement. What was that like?
It was not too long after Stonewall, so gay people

could finally be sort of open. And I really got into it. I was the office manager of Boulder Gay Liberation, I think the second and third years I was in college. Then I was also on the speakers' bureau. I spoke to a lot of abnormal-psychology classes, actually, on being gay. I tried to convince them that being gay was okay and that I didn't belong in an abnormal-psych class.

How did that go?
Pretty well. In all the speeches I gave—probably thirty or forty—I had only one openly hostile person.

It must have been very helpful for you, as well.
It was all part of the process you go through to prove that you're okay. Talking about it really helps, and it was a lot of fun.

A lot of younger gay people seem to think that the 1970s—before the AIDS crisis—was this magic time for gay people. Do you feel as if there was something about that period that we're missing now?
People always want to go back in time and say it used to be the golden age but that now it's all gone. There are things that are wonderful about being gay now that we didn't have then. There's a lot more support for relationships now than there

ever was then. I think that's a plus. Each time period is different. There are things I miss about the seventies, and there are things I don't miss.

Were there things you ever thought you couldn't do because you were gay?
Other than have a wife and kids, which I didn't want anyway, no. Shortly after I came out, my parents said, "You can't ever tell anyone about this because your father will lose his job." I knew that wasn't really true, but for several years I was fairly circumspect. I spoke on campus and places like that, but I didn't do newspaper interviews or anything.

When you moved into the business world, did you think it would be a drawback?
I worried about it for a long time. Not in a consuming way, but I worried about it. When the company was small, it didn't concern me at all. But then when all of a sudden I started to become more of a public figure within our industry—in the mid-eighties or so—I was always wondering what would happen if someone asked me if I was gay when I opened up audiences for questions. I was always wondering what I would do, and rehearsing what I would say. It turns out that no one ever asked, and the only time it comes up now is when I bring it up. My business is really technical, and

seldom in a technical conversation is the issue of being gay going to come up.

Have you ever felt that someone wouldn't work with you because of your sexuality and being so out?
It hasn't been too much of a problem. There was one division of a very large company that said they wouldn't order from us because I was gay. But mostly, it hasn't been a problem. I was actually kind of surprised by that. I was prepared for it to be a bigger problem.

Have you had any positive experiences within the industry from being out?
The thing that always makes me feel the best is when I make a speech and afterward someone comes up to me and thanks me for being out. That feels really good when it happens. That's one of the reasons I do it, to provide people with a role model, in the sense that I'm showing them they don't have to be as afraid as they think they have to be.

Two examples come to mind. One was someone who came up after a speech and was trying to thank me in this quiet voice for being gay and open about it. And I said, "It's really okay—you can say it." And then he spoke up, and said it loudly and proudly, and that was fun to see. The other was a speech I gave to the National Press

Photographers Association. I mentioned in passing that I had a boyfriend, and afterward a transgendered person, a woman who had become a man, came up to me and thanked me for coming out, because he felt so closeted and alone, and he was glad that someone would stand up in public in front of his peers and be gay, and that no one would care. He didn't know that no one would care. He thought it would be a problem. All of a sudden, he realized that it didn't have to be so bad.

It's unusual for businesspeople to come out so publicly. Did you get more attention because you're such a figure in the computer industry?
I got a lot of attention from the press because I came out right after Amendment 2—the amendment making it illegal to grant legal protection to people based on their sexual orientation—passed in Colorado. I hadn't planned it that way. But every year, we have a meeting in Colorado of all our major customers, and it happened that the meeting was scheduled for right after Amendment 2 passed. I had a couple of customers call and say they were boycotting Colorado because of it. And I said, "It's too late for me to change the meeting, but come, and we can vote on whether or not to move the meeting out of Colorado next year if the amendment goes into effect." So people came, and I gave a speech about what Amendment 2 was and what it

meant, and we voted. And except for two people—
who were from Colorado—everyone agreed to
boycott the state if the amendment went into
effect. That included people from a Baptist Sunday
school group, which I thought was fascinating.

I also said that one of the things Quark would do
was put at least a million dollars into the community to educate people about discrimination and
why that was a bad thing. But my customers are
people like the Associated Press, and afterward
they asked if they could run a story about what I
was doing. Then it just took off. At the time, openly gay men were not making million-dollar pledges
to gay causes in public, so we got some press attention from it.

How else are you involved in your community?
I have a foundation called the Gill Foundation. We
give away around a million and a half dollars a
year, primarily to gay causes, but also to children's
causes. I'm particularly interested in kids because I
think that if we don't have educated kids, ultimately our society is going to fail.

**Does it feel good to be able to influence things that
directly?**
Yes, but the things I'm doing aren't really that
direct. It's all the incredibly talented men and
women who are devoting their personal time to

the causes they believe in who are more important. The way I can help is by giving money so that these people can continue their work.

How do you think things have changed for gay people—especially young gay people—since you came out?
I think it's much easier to be gay in major metropolitan areas. There were no resources for gay youth when I was coming out. There were no gay youth groups, no community centers, nothing. In fact, the only organized gay groups were really those on college campuses. Now all these other kinds of resources are much more common.

What is most rewarding for you about being gay?
I think one of the things that gay people typically experience is that, because you are so oppressed in a sense from an early age, you become more introspective. You spend a lot of time thinking about yourself and who you are and what you want. And that's really a good thing. I'm sure there are easier ways to achieve that, but it's good nonetheless. I think because I did that as a kid, I learned more about myself a lot earlier on than people who just take their lives for granted.

What do you like best about being part of the gay community?

I think what I like is that it's so diverse. When you're straight, I think the tendency is to settle down into a community of people very much like yourself. But as a gay person, I have friends of many different types who do many different things. People in our community come from every possible walk of life, so it's impossible not to be exposed to different kinds of people. Yet at the same time, we have this one fundamental thing in common that brings us together.

What do you see as some of the challenges for young people coming out now?
The whole gay marriage issue. It was never even a consideration for me. Now it's a real possibility, and I have to think about it, both in personal terms and in terms of things like taxes and legal issues.

Would you do it?
I think Davol and I would. I struggled with it for a while. I kind of felt very free until the possibility of getting married came up. It was like, Okay, now you have to really, really commit. Ten years is a long time to be together, but this makes it all different. I think it will encourage people to get into long-term relationships. When I was younger, there wasn't much support for that.

What advice would you give to people just becoming part of the gay community?
What's ahead for you is whatever you want to get out of life. The main thing you have to worry about is that you're emerging from a period in your life where you feel very oppressed. And once you're out of that, there's a really strong temptation to go the other way and to do a lot of things to excess. It's okay to have a good time, but do things in moderation. And practice safer sex. I'm sure I'd say that.

THE GAY AND LESBIAN
COMMUNITY ON-LINE

If you want to find out more about the many lesbian and gay people involved in the computer
world, you might want to join Digital Queers, a
group of gay people interested in programming,
graphic design, and other aspects of the computer
industry. There are Digital Queers chapters
nationwide, and they can be found in the phone
book or in gay community newspapers. You can
also visit their site on the World Wide Web. It lists
all of the individual chapters and also supplies
links to other Web sites of interest to gay people.
The address of the Digital Queers site is www.dq.org.

If you have a computer and a modem, you might
also be interested in taking a look at some of the
many lesbian and gay sites on the World Wide
Web. This can be a great way to find information
about a wide variety of resources available to gay
people. If you are already familiar with using the
Web, try locating lesbian and gay sites by using the
search function on your Web browser.

If you aren't very familiar with using computers,
you might want to start out by visiting a gay community area of one of the large on-line service providers.
Three of the most popular services are listed below.
Each of these has a gay and lesbian forum. To order
the software necessary to connect with these on-line
services, call the numbers given below or write for

free software. Make sure that you indicate whether you have a Macintosh or a PC system.

America Online
8619 Westwood Center Drive
Vienna, VA 22182-2220
Phone: (800) 301-9966

One of the most popular on-line services, America Online has a gay and lesbian community forum featuring chat rooms, folders for virtually every interest, and a resource file of gay and lesbian organizations. Also featured is Lambda Rising bookstore's on-line area, where subscribers can order books, read reviews, and chat with authors.

CompuServe
5000 Arlington Centre Boulevard
P.O. Box 20212
Columbus, OH 43220
Phone: (800) 848-8990

Prodigy
44 South Broadway
White Plains, NY 10601
Phone: (800) PRODIGY

Similar to America Online, CompuServe and Prodigy feature various areas of interest to gay and lesbian people, including chat rooms and folders for various interest groups.

LESBIAN AND GAY FAST FACT **ELEVEN**

How Do I Find Other Gay Young People?

If you are a gay young person, you might feel all alone. Maybe you can't find other gay people, or anyone you feel comfortable talking to about the things you're thinking.

Many of us have had these feelings. It isn't easy sorting out everything we think and feel when we're trying to understand what being gay is and what it means for our lives. It is especially hard when we can't talk to our friends or our families about it.

Obviously, the best thing to do is try to find a support group. Fortunately, there are more and more of them available, usually through local lesbian and gay community centers. Some schools now offer them, as well. You can also try following the tips or contacting the groups listed on pages 235–237.

But maybe you just aren't able to find a support group, perhaps because you live in an area where there aren't any. If so, it may be harder to keep a positive attitude. But it isn't impossible. If you are a lesbian or gay young person who feels as though you'll never find other gay people, or be free to be happy, don't lose hope—someday you will! You might have to wait until you've finished school and can move to a place where there are other gay people, but it will happen.

In the meantime, there are things you can do to feel part of the gay community. You can read books about gay people. You can listen to music by gay people. You can watch movies about gay people. All of these things will help you see what a great community you belong to. And keep in mind that the people who wrote the books and composed the music and made the movies are people just like you. They probably felt the same way you do. Seeing what other gay people have done will help you imagine all the exciting things you could do, too.

SGT. EDGAR RODRIGUEZ
POLICE OFFICER

When many people think about the gay community, they think only about the people they see marching on television or the ones who are very visible because they work for gay organizations or gay causes. They don't always think about the many lesbian and gay people who work and live right in their communities, people they might come into contact with on a regular basis but never thought of as being gay.

In the same way, many gay and lesbian people believe that there are certain kinds of jobs they can't have, or things they cannot do, just because they are gay. They might believe that there are no other gay people doing those jobs, or that it would be too difficult to be a gay person in that field. Because they're afraid of what might happen, they miss out on doing something they really want to.

Sgt. Edgar Rodriguez is an example of a gay person who challenges both of those assumptions. As an openly gay officer in New York City's police department, he is able to show the people he comes into contact with through his work that gay people can be found in all walks of life.

As the president of the New York chapter of GOAL, the Gay Officers Action League, he also works to educate the police department about lesbian and gay issues, making it easier for other gay people who want to become involved in law enforcement to do so.

Did you always want to be a police officer?
I wanted to be a cop or a doctor, because those people were heroes to me, and I looked up to them. And I actually was involved in medicine, as an emergency medical technician, before I became a police officer.

Did you have any idea that you were gay when you were growing up?
I recognized that I was different, to the extent that I had a lot of thoughts and feelings that I was pretty sure my other friends did not have. They revolved around my strong affection for some of my male friends. Looking back on it now, I realize that I was having crushes on some of these guys. I remember trying to articulate my feelings for them and then realizing, through the responses of other people, that these kinds of feelings weren't acceptable, and weren't talked about. That caused me to go into some form of denial, where I tried to bury the feelings within myself.

Did you even know what being gay was?

Not really. I remember having these feelings and trying to figure them out, and what I ended up telling myself was that I was just looking for a best friend, someone I could hang out with, play sports with, and have fun with. I realize now that what I wanted was a lover, or what other people might look for in a girlfriend or boyfriend. But at the time, I didn't understand it.

Did you ever tell any of the friends you had these feelings for?
I was terrified to. I was sure that they would go and tell everyone else, and I knew that wouldn't be a good thing, even though I didn't really understand why.

What kinds of feelings did you have about gay people when you were growing up?
It was never really defined for me what being gay was. I didn't even really know the word *gay* when I was very young. When I did begin to hear it being talked about, it always had a derogatory connotation. To me, the word represented somebody who was ostracized, someone to be ashamed of, someone who was completely looked down upon. It was something that wasn't talked about, because it was an embarrassment.

At the same time, I didn't really understand what being gay was. All I knew was that it was something you didn't want to be. As I got older, I knew that it had to do with having sex with someone of the same sex, and that people thought this was a horrible thing to do. My first identification with what being gay was happened one night when I was watching the news. There was a story on about two gay men who had been killed. I remember that the first thing that went through my mind was, Why does anyone care? That's disturbing to me to think about now, but at the time, I had been given the impression that gay people weren't worth worrying about or caring about. I had been taught that in so many different ways. Maybe nobody ever told me that gay people were better off dead, but that's the message I received.

So that's what I thought being gay was—being an old man who did perverted things. I didn't know what those things might be, but I believed that it was some kind of sickness, and that these people didn't deserve to have someone care about them.

Did part of you think that you could never be gay because you just weren't like those people?
No doubt about it. I did not identify with being gay, because my definition of being gay was someone who was an older pervert or someone who wore pink dresses or leather, and I was not like that at all. I didn't think I could be gay, but I didn't

know what I was, because I still had these feelings.

How did that affect you as you got older?
I tried to hide the feelings I was having. I thought that maybe if I had lots of girlfriends, the feelings would go away. As a result, I started having sex with girls at a younger age than most of my friends did.

Did you think doing that would change you?
I didn't think it would change me, because I wasn't really trying to change. I didn't want to get rid of the feelings I was having; I wanted to prove to myself that I was like everyone else, and that probably everyone else was also having these feelings and just not talking about them. I wanted to think that it was normal.

Were you afraid that you couldn't be a police officer or anything else you wanted to be if you let anyone know what you were feeling?
I thought that making these feelings known to anybody would destroy my life completely, and that I couldn't be anything at all if people knew. Not just a cop, but anything. I was sure that I would be cast out and shamed if anyone knew.

How did you finally realize that what you were feeling had a name, and that you were gay?
It was a long series of little things that led up to it.

One of the breaking points came when I was in college. I went on a class trip to a museum. One of the curators there approached me and asked me if I wanted my own private tour. I said no, because I perceived him as being gay, and I didn't want people to see him near me. At the same time, as he walked away, I realized that I was attracted to him and I did want him to give me a private tour. I even waited around for him after everyone left, but I didn't see him.

That same week, I was driving through the city and I saw a man crossing the street. I looked at him, and I felt an attraction that I had never felt before. This man was everything I had ever dreamed about finding in another man physically, and it struck me so hard that I actually felt a hole in my chest. That was the first time I felt something for another man so strongly, and I knew I was experiencing something much different from the crushes I'd had on my friends in high school.

Did that change how you thought about yourself?
Not entirely. I still didn't think about being gay. I just knew that I had these very strong reactions to men. Then I got involved in the Police Academy, and I threw myself into all the work that was involved with that. I wasn't pursuing girls, but I wouldn't say I was gay, either. I even considered

becoming a priest, because I thought that would enable me just to forget about the problem by forcing me to be asexual. Instead, I buried myself in the police work. I was determined to excel, and I did very well.

When did you finally acknowledge what was going on with you?
After graduating from the academy, I went to work in the South Bronx. It was at that point, when I was about twenty-two years old, that I started to come to grips with it all. I had more time to think about things, because I wasn't studying or working to get through school. One night I was home, lifting weights, and I was thinking about it. I decided that I had to see a doctor or a therapist or someone I could talk to about the feelings I was having.

While I was lifting, I was listening to the radio. All of a sudden, the dj made this announcement saying, "If you want to hear more about the gay lifestyle, call the Gay Switchboard," and he gave the telephone number. I remember dropping the weights when I heard that. Something hit me, and I realized for the first time that there was actually a community of gay people, that there were people I could relate to and talk to. Hearing him say that number over the air made me understand that, because it sounded so normal for him to say it. I had never thought that before.

But you were living in New York City. How did you not know about the gay community?

I was in the South Bronx, and I was very insulated from the real world. The only times I came into contact with gay people were the few times I went into Manhattan with my friends, and I saw very stereotypical gay people. And of course I ran away from those kinds of people because I didn't think they and I could have anything in common.

Did you call the switchboard you heard about on the radio?

After I heard that radio announcement, I remember thinking, That's it. That's what I'm feeling. I'm gay. I sat down and just cried with relief, because finally I knew what was going on. It took that radio personality saying that one line to make me see that being gay was okay, that there were other people who were gay, and they even had this place you could call to talk about it.

I nervously called the hot line. It took me a couple of tries, because I kept hanging up. Finally, I talked to someone, and he told me that I wasn't alone, that there were many other people like me. Then I asked him where I could meet other people. New York didn't have a gay community center then, and he gave me the name of a gay bar.

Did you go?

I took the address and found it on a map. The next day, I went. I was so excited that I was going to do something new and wonderful for myself. I felt like I was on a journey to go meet gay people.

What was it like when you went in?
I walked past the bar a few times before I went in. I was afraid that the police department had cameras there, filming who went inside. But finally I walked in, and I was shocked to see all of these guys who were just like me. They all looked perfectly normal. I just watched and looked at people.

Then, all of sudden, a tremendous fear hit me. I realized that these were the people that other people were saying all of these bad things about. And if they were just like me, then I was one of the people that other people were saying bad things about. And that hurt. I was also angry that now I was one of the people that other people were trying to make out to be bad, because I knew I wasn't.

My life changed tremendously at that moment. I knew it would never be the same again, and that I would never go back. At the same time, I thought that I could never be honest again about who I was, because now I was one of the people everyone talked about.

Is that what you did—lead a double life?
That's exactly what I did. I had my gay friends and

my straight friends, and they never knew about one another. I never let the two worlds meet. When I went out to gay bars in the beginning, I used a fake name, and I told people I was an emergency medical technician, not a police officer. I even volunteered for a gay organization under a fake name, because I wanted very much to volunteer for a gay group, but I was afraid to be out.

How did you get to the point where you began not to be afraid?

It was really through that volunteer work, because that was where I began to grow, to learn more about myself and about other gay people. This was around the time that HIV and AIDS were really becoming a big issue in the community, and being a volunteer at a gay health center during that time helped me to learn a lot about the community. I met people from all different kinds of backgrounds, and I grew like I'd never grown before. It was like I went from being a small-town boy to a citizen of the world. It forced me to rid myself of a lot of my prejudices.

At the same time, I was learning a lot about prejudice from my job. Being Puerto Rican, I knew that there was prejudice against people, but I had never really experienced it. But when I started working as a police officer, I experienced a lot of prejudice from some of the other officers I worked with.

Did that make you even more nervous about coming out at work?

Definitely. I was having a hard enough time being accepted as a Puerto Rican cop in an almost all-white precinct station house. I couldn't even imagine what would happen if people at work knew I was gay.

Did you come out to your family?

I came out to my mother first. We were driving home from taking my cat to the vet, and I told her that there was something I wanted to talk to her about. I told her I was bisexual, which I guess I thought was easier than saying I was gay. Then I told her that the guy she thought was just a friend was someone I was dating. Then I handed her a box of tissues.

What did she do?

She threw the box of tissues back at me and said, "I don't need these." She suspected something was going on. She was a little angry, but she acted like it wasn't affecting her. But she told me not to tell my father.

Were you surprised by her reaction?

She pretended to be okay with it. Unbeknownst to me, she was spending every night crying about it and hurting for a long time. She suffered terribly because she thought that the son she loved so much was going to be ostracized by everyone who found out about his being gay, and she didn't want me to be hurt like that. I think she even felt that I would be better off dead than having to suffer the way she thought I would.

How did you help her understand what you were going through?
I began to realize that, now that she knew about me, she needed to be educated about what being gay meant. Just knowing I was gay wasn't enough. So I took her to a meeting of Parents and Friends of Lesbians and Gays. I got her some literature. Then I started taking her to gay functions so that she could see what my life was like and that the people I was with were happy.

What about your father?
My mother still didn't want me to tell him. But when she took a trip back to Puerto Rico, I decided I was going to tell him. I sat him down and told him that I loved him and that because he was my father, there was something I needed to tell him. I explained to him that I was gay, and that I was becoming more active in the community. I wanted him to know before he saw me in the media or found out by accident. I explained to him about the violence against gay people and how isolated

gay people were. I wanted him to understand, the way I had come to understand.

How did he react?

His first reaction was, "Being gay is very bad." But he listened to me, and in the end he said, "I love you, and what you are is what you are." I had learned by telling my mother how to educate him and to help him see why it was important for him to know about me and important for me to be out about who I was.

Did telling your family give you the courage you needed to come out on the job?

It gave me the foundation I needed. I needed my family to support me before I was able to go out there publicly. But the bulk of my support came from GOAL—the Gay Officers Action League—the organization for lesbian and gay police officers and criminal-justice professionals.

How did you become involved with GOAL?

I first heard about them back when I was in the Police Academy. One day, we had a visit from a sergeant, who made an announcement about this organization he was developing for lesbian and gay people in the criminal-justice field. He told us if we wanted more information, we could talk to him or go to another room for details. When he said that, the room fell silent, and all I could hear was the pounding of my heart and these faint snickers coming from the back of the room. I didn't know if it was for real. I even thought for a minute that maybe it was a setup to find out who was gay in the class.

Then my second thought was to wonder who this man was who was telling us about this organization. I thought that if he was gay, he had to have tremendous courage to come tell us all about himself, and about this group. The woman sitting next to me asked me what room he had said to go to, and I asked her why she was interested. She told me she was a lesbian, and I couldn't believe it. I didn't even really know what a lesbian was then.

So all of this was in my mind when I finally did decide to come out on the job. I ended up going to some GOAL meetings, but I was still scared. I was afraid to put my name on paper, and I ended up staying away from the group for a couple of years.

What brought you back?
The more I came out, the more I wanted to have other gay cops to talk to about my life. I started going to meetings once in a while, and I had fun hanging out with the other guys after meetings. We would just go out and have burgers and beers and talk. For the first time, I was doing what other cops

always did—sit around and talk about problems at work with other cops—but I was able to talk about being gay, too.

I was also accepted into a special unit of the police department, where I became a role model for children in the New York school system. I would go around and talk to school groups about drugs and peer pressure and self-esteem. And the more I did that, the more I realized that these kids really looked up to me.

At the same time, I was volunteering my off-duty time at an organization for lesbian and gay youth, and there I learned that there is a high rate of suicides and suicide attempts among gay youth, in part because they have no role models. It made me sad to realize that young people would try to destroy themselves because of their misconceptions about what being gay means and because no one was out there putting a face to the gay community for these kids. I saw that while I was going to schools and reaching a lot of kids in other ways, I wasn't reaching gay kids. That's when I realized that I had to come out, because I felt that as long as I and other gay people remained closeted, kids would keep killing themselves, and that as long as I was closeted, I would never be a whole person.

How did you come out to the people you worked with?

Around this time, the police department was starting a campaign to actively recruit lesbian and gay people onto the force. They were making a poster featuring gay police officers, and they needed models. So I decided to do it.

You came out by being on the poster?

Well, I thought that's what I was doing. What I didn't know was that the poster wasn't coming out for a couple of months. In the meantime, I still wasn't out at the office where I worked as part of the school visitation program. But whenever people brought up issues about racism or sexism or anything related to bigotry, I would also bring up homophobia. And people, I think, began to wonder why I did this. Then one day, I got into an argument with a woman at work, and she exploded at me. She started calling me a "faggot" and all kinds of things. Worst of all, she said something that I will never forget. She said, "And not only are you a faggot but you aren't even a proud faggot, because you're a closet case."

What did that do to you?

I was left speechless. I left work early, and driving back home, I just broke into tears. Because on some level, she was right. I knew that I wasn't fully prepared to come out, and that there were some good reasons for remaining in the closet at that time, but I also knew that as long as I did, I couldn't be who I wanted to be. The next day, I went in and told her that yes, I was gay, and that what she said had caused me tremendous pain.

What was her reaction?

She apologized to me. But she also went and told the whole office that I was gay. So suddenly everyone knew.

How did they treat you?

No one really said anything. That day, one by one, everyone left the office to do other things, until there was only one officer left. He was someone I admired very much, an African-American man who I thought was a great officer and role model. He was also a musician, and he came over to me and said, "Let me ask you something. I work with some gay musicians, and I just don't understand it. Can you explain it to me?" Well, I sat with him for two hours, and I told him everything I had ever experienced about being gay. When I was done, he stood up and shook my hand, and he thanked me for helping him understand. And he told me that he respected me so much for coming in every day with a smile on my face while I was carrying around the burden of not being able to talk about who I was. I realized that I had educated this man. By talking to him, I helped him understand something he hadn't understood before. That's when I understood that my purpose in life was to teach people about this issue.

It seems like everything in your life was coming together to lead you in that direction. Is that how it worked out?
Shortly after this all happened, I was promoted to sergeant, and I changed offices. And of all the places I could have been assigned, I ended up in the Sixth Precinct, right in the middle of Greenwich Village. I was right in the middle of New York's gay community.

What was it like working there?
Well, no one there knew I was gay when I first arrived. It wasn't that when I came out at my old office, suddenly the whole New York City police department knew. I decided that I was going to have a hard enough time being the new sergeant, and being Puerto Rican, without adding coming out to it. So I decided to wait. And things went really well. I got along with people, and they liked me. Then, about a month later, the recruitment poster I'd posed for came out. I'd forgotten all about it. The property clerk in our office got it, and he showed it to everyone. So all of a sudden, everyone knew I was gay.

And what happened?
Even in a precinct within a large gay community the people there are still cops, and they still have their individual prejudices. When you're a cop, it's possible to work within a community of people totally unlike yourself and never learn anything about those people. It isn't until you work with them or make the effort to learn about them and understand them that you change and that you learn what their issues are. That's why it's so important to bring diversity into the police department. Many of the cops in the Sixth Precinct worked with a community of gay people every day, but they still didn't have any idea what it was like to be gay, so they didn't know how to deal with me. It's one thing having to work in a gay community, but working for a gay supervisor is something altogether different. They didn't know what I might be dealing with, or what issues I might have to face. So the education started all over again.

Did anyone have a problem with you?
Yes, some people did. A small percentage of them were homophobic, and they began to challenge my authority and my ability to supervise them. Many of these people were the same ones who challenged me because I was Puerto Rican.

What about the gay community—did you have

problems with them because you were a cop and were perceived by some to be the enemy?

Oh, yes. It was a double whammy. And many times I was caught in the middle. This was the time, in the mid-1980s, when there were a lot of rallies and demonstrations by gay activist groups, and often I would be out there as a police officer and gay people would come up and scream at me, calling me a homophobe and saying I hated gays. Then, when I would tell them I was gay, they would say I was the enemy because I was a police officer.

What did you tell them?

I told them that I was trying to change things from within by being a part of it and by educating people. Some people were proud of me for that; others still thought I was a traitor. There were gay people who would confront me when I was volunteering in my off-duty hours and give me a hard time about working for the police.

How did you deal with being on both sides?

It was very hard. Many times, I would be in the middle, and I would have to be honest. Sometimes I sided with the gay community, and sometimes I sided with the cops, depending on who I felt was right. People always wanted me to take sides, and I didn't want to. At the same time, I was still dealing with coming out, so I had all those added pressures.

How did that affect you?

The result was that for a while I couldn't do anything right. There were rumors following me, and people would question my decisions. But I just had to do my job and try to keep things in balance. It was hard, because I was angry about homophobia, so when I encountered it in another cop, I would be even tougher on that person. That didn't make me a lot of friends at work.

Did you feel as if everyone expected you to know everything and be perfect?

Yes, and that's what made it the hardest. I was supposed to know everything about being gay and about being a police officer dealing with the gay community. But I was still learning about myself and trying to figure out how to make everything work the best way possible. I learned a lot about dealing with people because of those experiences.

I feel that I made some significant accomplishments at the Sixth Precinct. I left there somewhat frustrated over the few officers who made working there a bit more difficult than it might have been, but I was satisfied with the impact I made on all of the officers' prejudices about lesbian and gay people. My visibility did a lot to help other gay and lesbian officers come out of the closet and be prouder of who they are. Being out also allowed me to help lesbian and gay hate-crime victims come forward who would have otherwise never reported these incidents to the police because of mistrust. These accomplishments alone were worth any aggravation I suffered.

Now I have a different kind of job. I work in an office setting within the police department. And I use what I learned back then to help me approach people in a way that lets me educate them without being angry at what they don't know.

What's the hardest part about being a gay cop?

Not everyplace is going to have the foundation built to make it a welcoming place for gay and lesbian officers to work. So for every cop who comes out, it's going to be a different experience.

Do you think it's important for gay officers to come out?

One of the biggest lessons I've learned from my journey is that there are certain things that will make you more vulnerable and cause you more harm than others. The biggest one is remaining closeted. Because as long as you're not out, you will always be in an isolated position where you may compromise your ability to respond effectively to homophobia, either against yourself or against others. You are also more likely not to take protective action for yourself or someone else in situations where being gay is a factor—such as hate crimes—because of your fear of being outed or associated with being gay. This alone can make you less effective as an officer. I have known too many gay and lesbian officers who held out to the last possible second to get help in dealing with a problem because they were afraid that asking might result in their being outed, with the result that the problems they were facing became much worse than they needed to be.

Being closeted also puts you in a position where people feel that they can discriminate against you if they find out that you are gay. If you remain silent, you won't have the resources, including other gay officers and straight allies, that would otherwise be available to you. If you are out and show the world that you are sure of yourself, people will be less likely to try to cause problems for you. Most homophobes know that closeted people are much more vulnerable than those who are out and proud of who they are. Because once you're out, they can't use the threat of outing you as a weapon to hurt you.

What would you say to gay people who are the victims of antigay hate crimes but who are afraid to go to the police because they don't trust them?
Many gay people have been treated badly by the police. That's another reason why it's so important for gay officers to come out. Not only does it begin

to change from within the way the police department looks at the gay community but it also gives the community a way to connect to the police that they might not have otherwise. I know many people who came to the police for help because they knew they had a friend there in me. It's all about visibility. Because once people know that there's a gay person in the department, it changes everything, both for the people on the inside and for the people on the outside.

Is who you are now, and the way your life is now, anything you could have imagined when you were first at the Police Academy?
Not in a million years. This is why people have to be educated. They have to understand that the tremendous fear that grips them when they're first coming to terms with who they are will go away. It will dissipate over time, until one day they can look back and won't believe they ever had that fear. Back when I was a new recruit, I could never even have considered being in GOAL. Now I'm the president of the New York chapter, which is the largest one in the country.

How does that feel?
It's wonderful to realize that what I'm doing is impacting people's lives in a way that's so good, and so important. It's nothing I could stop doing,

even if I tried, and it's something I couldn't have imagined doing in a million years back when I was terrified of even thinking the word *gay*.

Today I am happy and proud of who I am. I am especially proud of being gay. It has made my life an incredible journey. It has brought me joy and pain, and these experiences have helped make me who I am today. If I had a chance to live my life over again, I wouldn't do it any other way.

I'm happiest because I'm changing the way people think—both in the gay community and in the police community—and I never believed I was capable of doing something like that. Growing up, I had so many fears and doubts about myself. Never did I imagine that I would be able to face so many of the fears I had and turn them around so that they made a difference in my life and in the lives of others. *¡Gracias a la vida!*

If you are a gay person thinking of becoming involved in law enforcement, or want to find out more about lesbian and gay people in the police and criminal-justice fields, you can get information about these topics from the Gay Officers Action League. There are GOAL offices in many cities around the country, so look in your local white pages to see if there is an office near you. You can also contact GOAL's New York City office and ask them to help you find the branch closest to you. The address:

Gay Officers Action League (GOAL)
P.O. Box 2038
Canal Street Station
New York, NY 10013
Phone: (212) NY1-GOAL (691-4625)

You can also access the GOAL New York Web site. It describes upcoming GOAL functions and activities, lists the other GOAL groups around the country, and provides links to other organizations involved in lesbian and gay issues within the law-enforcement and criminal-justice fields. The address of the site is www.geocities.com/~goal.ny/.

FOR FURTHER INFORMATION
SOURCES OF HELP AND INFORMATION

The Gay and Lesbian National Hot Line
If you are a lesbian or gay young person and you need information about gay issues, or if you just need someone to talk to, you can call the Gay and Lesbian National Hot Line. GLNH is a nonprofit organization that provides nationwide toll-free peer counseling, information, and referrals. The hot line is open Monday through Friday from 6:00 P.M. to 10:00 P.M. and Saturday from noon to 5:00 P.M., eastern standard time. The phone number is (888) THE-GLNH (843-4564).

On-Line Help
There are numerous sites on the World Wide Web that provide information for lesbian and gay young people. Because these sites change so frequently, it is impractical to list them here. There are, however, some long-running sites that provide links to other areas on the Web. One of the most comprehensive of these is Rainbow Youth Links, which provides information on gay student organizations across

the country and has lists of resources to help young people connect with the gay community. The address of the site is www.youthweb.com/rainbow/.

Finding Local Groups

The best way for you to get information about gay and lesbian groups in your area is to call your local lesbian and gay community center. Many cities have these centers, and they are usually listed in the white pages of the phone book. You may also try looking in the Yellow Pages under the heading *Gay.* If you find that a phone number or hot line is no longer in service, contact another organization and find out what else is available in your area. If you cannot find anything listed under *Gay or Lesbian Services,* you might try calling a women's center or health clinic. They may be able to refer you to a group.

Another excellent way to locate gay groups in your area is to pick up a copy of a gay newspaper or magazine. These can be found at lesbian and gay bookstores, at women's bookstores, and often at local video stores, restaurants, or gift stores. These papers will usually contain listings for groups that meet in your area.

If you do not have a local gay and lesbian community center and cannot find any listings for gay organizations in your area, a good organization to contact is Parents and Friends of

Lesbians and Gays. PFLAG operates more than three hundred groups around the country, offering support to lesbian and gay people and their families, and it can help you locate other useful groups in your area. You can reach this organization at:

PFLAG
1101 14th Street NW, Suite 1030
Washington, DC 20005
Phone: (202) 638-4200
World Wide Web: www.pflag.org
E-mail: info@pflag.org

You might also want to get a copy of *You Are Not Alone: National Lesbian, Gay, and Bisexual Youth Organization Directory.* It can be ordered from the Hetrick-Martin Institute, 2 Astor Place, New York, NY 10003; phone: (212) 674-2400. The Hetrick-Martin Institute is devoted to serving gay, lesbian, bisexual, and transgendered young people, and it may be able to provide information on groups for young people in your area.

INDEX

AIDS, 38, 86, 88, 109, 114–15, 124–26, 154, 197, 218
  books on, 126
American Psychiatric Association, 27
Annie on My Mind (book), 48–49, 51, 60–66

bisexual people, 5, 144, 147, 237
Bryant, Anita, 185–86

censorship, 48–49, 55, 63–66
children of gay people, 127–39
  adoption of, 20, 88, 127–28, 132–34
  books on, 139
  in divorce, 127
Clinton, Bill, 176
Colorado's Amendment 2, 200–201
comic strips, 10, 17–22
  list of, 23–24
coming out
  how to do it, 190–92
  meaning of, 165–67
computer on-line services, 205–6, 235–36

"Dykes to Watch Out For" (comic strip), 10, 18, 22

families, gay. *See* children of gay people
Frasier (TV sitcom), 73, 82

Galindo, Rudy, 44
Gay and Lesbian National Hot Line (GLNH), 235
gay bars, 216–18
gay community, 5
  AIDS and, 124–26
  books on, 121–23, 192
  on-line, 205–6, 235–36
  support groups in, 207
gay community centers, how to find, 236
Gay Games, 43
gay health center, 218
gay history book for high school students, 178–79
gay marriage, 134, 203
gay roles, gay actors for, 82–83
gays and lesbians
  basic books on, 9, 192
  groups for reform of, 28
  how people know whether they are, 70–72
  how to find, 207–8, 235–37

meaning of terms, 7–9
negative images of, 31, 35, 38, 41, 65, 88–90, 110–13, 211–12
number of, 45–47
stereotypes about, 106–8
teaching about, in schools, 168–69
why some people are, 25–28
Gay Switchboard (New York City), 215
gene, "gay," 26
Gill Foundation, 201
GLAAD (Gay and Lesbian Alliance Against Defamation), 90–91
GLSEN (Gay, Lesbian, Straight Education Network), 169, 176, 177, 183, 189
GLSTN (Gay, Lesbian, Straight Teachers Network), 172, 175–76
GOAL (Gay Officers Action League), 210, 221–22, 232, 234

Hall, Radclyffe, 55–56
homophobia, 87–91, 181
  censorship and, 66
  hate crimes against gays, 229–32
  in Hollywood, 82
  in police department, 227, 229, 230
  in pro boxing, 33
  in schools, 173, 175
homosexuality, not personality disorder, 27–28

Jewish tradition, lesbian rabbi in, 144, 146, 148–58

lesbians. *See* gays and lesbians
Louganis, Greg, 43–44

Massachusetts, Equal Education law in, 173–74
McCarthyism, 116
military service, gays in, 111
Mosca, Frank, 48
movies, 13–14, 85–86, 90

Navratilova, Martina, 44
newspapers and magazines, 18, 92–93, 99–105, 179–80, 236
  list of, 104–5
novels, 55–56, 59–60, 128
  list of, 67–69

Olympics, gays and, 29–30, 32, 33–34, 43–44
One magazine, 179–80
Only Thing Worse You Could Have Told Me, The (one-man show), 73, 75–76, 79
Out magazine, 92–93, 99–103, 105

Pallone, Dave, 43

Parents and Friends of Lesbians and Gays (PFLAG), 220, 236–37

Quark (company), 193, 201
queer, use of word, 5–6, 130

religions, 140–58, 178
    list of gay religious groups, 159–64
    "reform" of gays by, 28
role models, gay and lesbian, 40–41, 94, 110, 166, 185, 187, 199, 222
    actor as, 73–84
    business executive as, 193–204
    cartoonist as, 10–22
    educator as, 168–88
    magazine editor as, 92–103
    medical doctor as, 109–20
    mother as, 127–39
    Olympic boxer as, 29–42
    police officer as, 209–33
    rabbi as, 143–58
    writer as, 48–66, 127–39

schools
    gay-straight alliances at, 174, 189
    gay teachers in, 168–69, 171–76, 184–87
    teaching of gay issues in, 168
self-image, 39, 40, 42
sports, gays and, 29–36
    books on, 43–44
stereotypes, 106–8
Stonewall riots (1969), 196
suicide among gay youth, 222

therapy, 27–28, 97–98, 112–13, 195–96
transgendered people, 5, 200, 237
TV shows, 73, 88, 90

Womanews (newspaper), 18
Word Is Out (film and book), 13–14